8 UNIVERSAL LAWS

"Fer Broca is a true seeker, journeying across distant lands and deep within himself. In this luminous book, he generously shares the wisdom he has gained from the intersection of the visible and invisible worlds. Through eight universal laws and accessible practices, Broca invites us to step beyond limitations into a life of limitless possibility. This book is an inspiring guide for anyone longing to cultivate lasting peace, renewed hope, and genuine joy."

ANURADHA DAYAL-GULATI, PH.D. AUTHOR OF
HEAL YOUR ANCESTRAL ROOTS

8 UNIVERSAL LAWS

EXERCISES AND MEDITATIONS FOR SELF-REALIZATION

FER BROCA

Translated by
VICTORIA ROJAS

Destiny Books
Rochester, Vermont

Destiny Books
One Park Street
Rochester, Vermont 05767
www.DestinyBooks.com

Destiny Books is a division of Inner Traditions International

Originally published in Spanish in 2025 by Inner Traditions en Español under the title *8 Leyes Universales: Guía para alcanzar la penitud.*

Cataloging-in-Publication Data for this title is available from the Library of Congress

ISBN 979-8-88850-227-3 (print)
ISBN 979-8-88850-228-0 (ebook)

Printed and bound in the United States by Lake Book Manufacturing, LLC

10 9 8 7 6 5 4 3 2 1

Text design and layout by Debbie Glogover
This book was typeset in Garamond Premier Pro with Gill Sans MT Pro, Le Monde Sans Std and Span used as display typefaces

To send correspondence to the author of this book, mail a first-class letter to the author c/o Inner Traditions • Bear & Company, One Park Street, Rochester, VT 05767, and we will forward the communication.

To joy, kindness, love, wisdom and peace.
These are also essential laws.
What you'll be is what you do now.

BUDDHA

Contents

Prologue

An Invitation

In deep knowledge lies the key that opens the doors to total fulfillment.

My heart pounded, not with fear but with excitement for what was about to happen—the day had arrived . . .

A colorful walk awaited me as I slowly strolled over countless cobblestones steeped in history. "I'm here." My mind couldn't settle down during my walk. Of course, it couldn't be otherwise, with the Seine's breeze caressing my face as if confirming that everything I was seeing was real. I was in Paris!

I felt so happy and grateful to the universe, for what I was experiencing was not a mirage. I reached a row of tourists and stood at the back, counting the steps left to enter. Finally, I had before me the majestic cathedral that I had contemplated so many times in photographs, and I was moments away from fulfilling one of the greatest dreams of my childhood—to see Notre Dame.

There I stood before that imposing structure—so sober, so beautiful, so mystical, so absurdly attractive. It had been inviting me for years to witness its power, materialized by subtle forces and ancestral wisdom. Its sculpted façade deserved to be contemplated for a long time. However, the queue moved forward and, in less time than expected, I had already crossed through one of the three magnificent entrance doors.

At that moment I was fully aware of being in a space filled with hidden messages, revealed only to those who know how to perceive beyond the obvious. With my mind and soul ready to listen, my feet advanced over the flagstones of the temple, where time seemed to have stopped. My eyes were enthralled by the grandeur of more than a thousand stained-glass windows, and woven domes that seemed to touch the sky.

I made the tour wrapped in the solemnity of sacred sound. I admired the colorful stained-glass windows, the small sculptures, the delicacy of the art. . . . Suddenly, I arrived at a small enclosure that made me shudder—a chapel dedicated to the Virgin of Guadalupe.

In the blink of an eye, the image of Mexico's great mother transported me back to my homeland, and I became once again the innocent neighborhood kid I once was—a seven-year-old boy sifting through magazines and calendars in search of treasures, my hand marking the course of the scissors, enjoying cutting out photographs of the most beautiful palaces and churches in the world.

Back then, I delighted in traveling through my dreams, and to that end I had become an explorer of images that captured my attention. There were many of them, but I primarily chose those for which I felt a special attraction or connection. Whenever I found one, I would carefully cut it out and reverently place it on the walls of my room. I didn't know it at the time, but that selection of images would mark the spiritual path of my life, and would lead me to find myself in places and countries that at the time seemed unattainable to me.

My parents watched me with a mix of emotion and disbelief. To them, my dreams were just the fantasies of a young boy, innocent illusions that would inevitably crumble when confronted with the harsh realities of life. This was their belief, instilled in them over the years. It seemed simply impossible that a child like me could achieve such distant dreams.

Many people believe that those of us from humble backgrounds, with limited financial resources, cannot achieve great things. But I thought differently. Something inside told me those places I had somehow chosen were waiting for me—among them, the legendary building I was currently exploring. I had envisioned it since childhood, and now, as an adult, that long-held dream was materializing before my eyes.

As I had eagerly read Victor Hugo's work, I hoped to encounter Quasimodo among the cathedral's gargoyles, just as vividly portrayed in his timeless novel, *The Hunchback of Notre Dame.*

I recall my childhood as being marked by an insatiable curiosity and an unquenchable thirst for knowledge. This is why I adored immersing myself in my grandfather's books. Expeditions to remote ruins, explorations of castles, enigmatic monuments, ancient civilizations. I would close my eyes and imagine myself traversing these landscapes with utter delight. I could even smell them, feel the wind, envision the trees, and connect with the earth. "I will be there someday," I would tell myself time and time again, savoring those moments.

"That's a long way off," and "getting there costs a fortune," they would say at home. I would listen in silence as the adults affirmed these things. According to them, we belonged to a world that prevented us from having such expectations. However, a voice within me, a deep-seated force, fought against this idea and opened me up to believing it was indeed possible.

The fact is, like many people, I grew up in a belief system where a great many things were labeled "impossible." Thus, as a child, I accepted as normal the idea that air travel and exploring castles were unattainable luxuries. We simply couldn't even afford to dream.

"Don't get your hopes up, Fer. That's for others." But I didn't stop hoping for the opposite. I had a tremendous curiosity to discover what lay beyond what could be seen. And that drive increased when I started experiencing visions and premonitions.

Discovering this gift in myself was very complex because I had no way of talking about it or developing it without being questioned and judged.

I was raised in a Catholic Christian family, with conservative, very provincial customs, and that environment made it difficult for me to understand and live with my "special" abilities. I received many warnings and scoldings for expressing how I perceived some things, which was in a very unconventional way. Despite everything, I kept my particular perception of the world.

For me, it was common to feel that when something happened there were hidden threads moving to make it happen. That hunch pushed me to explore, to investigate, to read even more.

From an early age, I walked around with a book or a *Selecciones* magazine (the Mexican version of *Reader's Digest*) under my arm. As a teenager, I began to delve into more advanced spiritual topics. My grandfather, being the Mason that he was, had a library with very old tomes related to the esoteric and the mystical. I was captivated by it.

At the age of twelve, I ended up reading a book complex for my age: *Reincarnation*, by Papus. Upon reaching the last page of this book, my life changed. I understood that behind my apparent social limitations and economic restrictions lay a universe of possibilities that could break through any barrier, no matter how impenetrable it seemed.

At the age of thirteen I began to perform my first conscious visualizations and to formulate decrees, which I now recognize were quite poorly done. My methods were simple, as I was just a beginner, a high-school boy. Fortunately, an unforgettable teacher crossed my path, who would mark a true turning point in my life. It was my Spanish teacher who introduced me to readings that untied the knots of my thinking in relation to chakras, meditation, and mantras.

This teacher, with marked spiritual inclinations, spoke to me about the practice of meditation and the functioning of the universe's energies. Conversing with him was a tremendous revelation that propelled me and gave me the encouragement to delve deeper into these and other topics related to the forces of the universe. He allowed me to understand that what I sensed indeed existed, and that, in addition, these phenomena had been studied since ancient times.

It was a great relief to know that at least one respectable adult (not a charlatan) was interested in the matters that captivated me. During that period I began to discover that there are invisible links between the world we see and the world of energies, and that those energies intervene in everything we do.

As I grew older it became more difficult for me to coexist with the limiting ideas that had been instilled in me since I was a child. These heavy paradigms suffocated me like a straitjacket and obstructed my personal growth. I realized many approaches were negatively conditioning my thinking and my way of acting, and I wanted to get rid of that. My search led me to discover that the universe was expanding infinitely, far beyond what I had been taught.

Driven by an insatiable curiosity that has remained with me to this day, I embarked on a serious exploration of various topics including alternative healing techniques, the power of meditation, the power of the mind, and the practice of Reiki.

I dedicated myself wholeheartedly, made many sacrifices, and disciplined myself to achieve my goals. I even saved up for months to take classes on universal energy and learn about the chakras. It was all worth it, as I found complete fulfillment and happiness by pursuing this path of knowledge.

Upon turning eighteen, I was summoned by a great spiritual master who invited me to Chiapas to continue my training under his guidance. It was a true honor to become a disciple of this remarkable being, from whom I learned so much and whom I still call Master with respect and admiration to this day.

Around that same time I decided to embark on a teaching journey, as I realized it was time to share my learnings with others who had the same desire to grow and improve their lives. I started with a small group that eventually grew larger. Today, we are thousands walking this path together.

I came to understand the immense power that comes with sharing wisdom, as well as applying mystical knowledge and the Universal Laws, which you will learn more about later.

As I implemented my learnings, I watched with awe as new opportunities blossomed in my life. The deeper I delved into practice, the more I grasped the underlying principles of the cosmic interplay of energies. However, manifesting Universal Laws requires personal effort. With this understanding, I dedicated myself to refining and perfecting their application within myself first. Through this practice, I reached a level where events once deemed impossible by many began to materialize.

And so, sooner than I expected, the energies and forces of the universe aligned to give me enormous gifts—among them, to visit the sites that made up my collection of cherished childhood images.

That same boy who had been told it was unthinkable went to visit the Notre Dame Cathedral, Tibet, Egypt, the Vatican, and traveled to Machu Picchu—he even toured castles all over Europe. I also made memorable trips to remote places, like India, New Zealand, Vietnam, Bhutan, and Iceland. So far, I have managed to visit more than eighty-five countries, crossing the seven seas and traveling across the five continents.

Among my many childhood experiences, I used to go with my dad to a small hill in Praderas de San Mateo, through Lomas Verdes, in the State of Mexico. It was like a kind of lookout point with a beautiful view of the whole city. My father would often say to me, "You see, Fer, I'm going to buy a piece of land right here." Twenty-five years went by, and my father's dream remained unfulfilled.

Nevertheless, the seed of that dream was sown within me, and I could see it sprout. On my thirty-second birthday, I managed to buy an apartment on a high floor of a building built precisely on that small hill. Every day, upon waking up, I could enjoy that incredible view and that privileged location.

No one in my family would have thought I could live in such a place; however, it happened.

All these achievements and many more arose as a result of putting Universal Laws into practice. I learned some of these laws from my teachers, others on my travels, and others on my own, recognizing ancestral wisdom.

Universal Laws are a legacy of the wisdom of ancient cultures highly advanced in spiritual matters, which have developed across different times and spaces. Many philosophical and mystical currents around the world converge in the practice of these essential and true principles.

While I have delved into and applied a vast array of these laws, I have undertaken a meticulous selection of those I believe to be the most transformative and empowering. I have chosen those that have the greatest relevance in everyday life and yield the most remarkable results. These precious laws, which I now share with you, stem from my heart, my studies, my thoughts, my reflections, my introspection, my practice, and my extensive journey of knowledge and experience.

Over the years, I have incorporated the principles of these Laws into my actions, thoughts, and specific life circumstances, and I can affirm with full responsibility that when applied correctly from a place of consciousness and love, they inevitably work.

Thanks to the practice of these principles, I am a happy person today. I have a fulfilling life sustained by values, convictions, and very clear goals. Everything I do and share is governed by consciousness, peace, and harmony.

For more than two decades I have dedicated myself to accompanying thousands of people in their transformation processes, and have witnessed their incredible evolution both spiritually and materially, as well as in the personal, collective, family, and social spheres.

I have also had the pleasure of being able to positively influence the lives of those who wish to awaken. To do this, I have used various means such as radio, television, publishing books, and the many workshops, courses, trips, retreats, and conferences I have given around the world.

I am deeply grateful for the life I've built. The work I do and the connections I forge with others bring me fulfillment. I am content with who I am today, and I cherish the harmonious and peaceful space I share with my wonderful family.

Through meditation, reflection, and dedicated study I've gained access to powerful knowledge on cultivating fulfillment and abundance. This knowledge is distilled into the eight Universal Laws I share with you here. By embracing these principles, you too can tap into the universe's wellspring of happiness and abundance.

I invite you to take a step forward and consciously prepare yourself by learning, practicing, and applying these laws to unlock the fulfilling life you deserve.

Allow me to guide you on this beautiful path of evolution and awakening.

The basic laws of the universe are simple,
but because our senses are limited,
we can't grasp them.

Albert Einstein

Introduction to the Universal Laws

Universal Laws govern everything you know . . . and everything you don't.

Can you imagine transforming everything you've ever dreamed of being or possessing into reality? Now imagine that this idea is no longer part of your imagination, but a factual, tangible element, the product of your dedication and loving creation. But, how is this alchemy of dreams into something real possible? You will find the answer here.

We are all on a journey of transformation, a path where applying what you learn is key. These pages won't offer rules for saints, guidelines for mystics, or doctrines for ascetics. Instead, they present principles, Universal Laws that are meant for everyone.

Universal Laws are principles we all need to know and apply in order to live better.

Beginning this book proved a daunting task. The sheer volume of Universal Laws I encountered threatened to overwhelm me. My initial list stretched beyond seventy. Yet, my objective wasn't simply to present theoretical knowledge. I aimed to equip readers with practical tools seamlessly integrated into their daily lives, fostering abundance. Thus, a more judicious approach seemed necessary. I selected the principles I deemed truly fundamental to solidifying one's understanding of the Universal Laws.

From this vast repository of ancient wisdom, I distilled eight cornerstone keys. These keys are not isolated entities; each principle serves as the parent of the next, giving rise to its successor, weaving everything into a web of interconnected laws.

The Universal Laws expounded in this book draw upon diverse spiritual traditions, each possessing an evolutionary lineage. When I speak of evolution, it is crucial to remember that Christianity, Islam, and Buddhism have all undergone transformations over time. While most doctrines address similar themes, their approaches vary considerably.

Love, compassion, forgiveness, and mercy—these themes resonate across spiritual traditions worldwide. It's ironic that, despite being preached for centuries in diverse cultures, these virtues remain largely unpracticed due to our inability to embody them consciously and connect them to their divine source. Once we grasp that our supplications should be directed to the Higher Power, regardless of its name or form, optimal outcomes will follow. A wealth of profound teachings can be found in shamanism, Hinduism, Sufism, Judaism, Christianity, Islam, and all spiritual traditions. In exploring each principle, I will draw upon the words and concepts of the tradition that most reveres that particular principle, honoring the spiritual current that places the greatest emphasis on that specific law.

The Universal Laws and their principles govern the flow, movement, energy, and vibration of everything. When we say "everything," we refer to the collective consciousness, encompassing all that you see, know, and perceive. They also govern all that you are unaware of or unable to perceive.

In their eagerness to be perceived as sages, some may believe they grasp the entirety of the Universal Laws. However, this is a misconception. How can one truly comprehend a principle that is constantly evolving?

A less abstract example might be that of a lawyer who studied in Spain but thought he could litigate in France just because he knew Spanish law in its entirety. The absurdity is clear. Legal systems differ significantly, rendering expertise in one irrelevant in the other. Just as no lawyer can claim complete knowledge of the law, no one can definitively claim to understand the totality of the Universal Laws.

When I speak of Universal Laws, I mean the totality of totality—not of mine or yours but of all existing and understood realities. Universal Laws serve everyone, both for your neighbor in Mexico in 2022 and for the princesses in India in the twelfth century. Will they also be useful for you? Yes, they will. What makes you think they only favor a few, a small niche, and that you cannot benefit from them? Remember that, despite your lack of knowledge, the laws also govern everything you ignore. Therefore, the Universal Laws will serve you, your children, and your grandchildren, no matter if they are explained on an iPad or written on ancient parchment, no matter if they are hieroglyphics from an Egyptian scroll or taught by a philosopher in a square in Athens. These laws are universal, whether we are aware of them or not.

They are not subject to referenda or votes; they are simply what they are. We may or may not understand them, but their nature is absolute. The Universal Laws encompass everything. Therefore, when we study it, it takes us out of our box or out of our comfort zone, transcending our limited perception of reality.

The fact that a person does not know sun exposure burns the skin does not exclude them from getting burned if they remain a long time exposed to sunlight. The fact that a person does not know speeding is considered an offense in a foreign country will not exempt them from a speeding ticket. Again, the fact that we are unaware of the Universal Laws does not free us from their influence, their presence, their mandate, or their life force.

To elaborate on several of these laws, I will draw upon philosophical and spiritual teachings from the Vedic tradition of India. With roots dating back five thousand years before Christ, the Vedic tradition stands as one of the world's oldest. This means that before philosophy as we know it existed, Hindus were already working on matters of spiritual development.

There is a succession of spiritual principles that come from shamanistic traditions, which later mutated into Brahmanism, and were finally converted into another school of philosophy within Hinduism, known as Vedanta.

In Hindu creation myths, the universal spirit, Brahma, is depicted as lacking any needs. This portrayal challenges the common assumption that a divine creator necessitates a grand plan for humanity. We might imagine ourselves fulfilling some cosmic purpose, but this perspective overlooks the inherent creativity of the divine. The divine creative energy doesn't require humans; its existence doesn't hinge on our justification. Perhaps our creation stemmed from serendipity, a universe at play. Think of an artist before a blank canvas, brimming with colors and brushes, playfully making strokes. The resulting masterpiece wasn't commissioned but born from a sense of playfulness.

Yes, for Hindus creation is a game, and it's far from over. Every day, creation unfolds anew, offering each new soul opportunities for learning and growth.

This original presence, this central source of energy, continues to create, continues to manifest itself—it remains in play. And, as with any game, there are rules to follow if one wishes to continue playing. In other words, creation is ongoing—and this is the foundation of how and why Universal Laws function.

When we grasp the vastness of the universe, its unfixed and limitless nature, we discover our own agency within it. No longer passive observers, we can become active participants, co-creators shaping the ever-present reality. This empowers us to design a future aligned with our aspirations.

Imagine a house under construction. Until it is complete, changes remain readily achievable. Walls can be painted, tapestries hung, floors installed, or even walls moved entirely. However, once the house is finished, the desire for transformation requires demolition—tearing down existing structures to make way for desired modifications. In the same way, the universe is perpetually "under construction," as the expansive movement of creation continues.

According to the Vedas, Upanishads, and Hindu canons, the universe unfolded through an inhalation of creative energy, followed by an exhalation that birthed light.

According to some astrophysicists who study the creation of the universe (cosmology), there was once a contraction of the universe

(Big Bang) in which energy was condensed at a single point in space. This energy then exploded, and its expansion at the energy level has not yet ceased. In this sense, the universe continues in a constant state of exhalation, creating new planets, emitting new vibrations, generating all existing possibilities, even those we do not yet imagine.

Thus, the presence of the divine spirit in creation is so potent, its exhalation, its spirit, continues to expand and create. Think of the word "spirit" as meaning "wind" or "breath." With this definition, it is easier to understand how this spirit continues its creative work. Now, if you can align yourself with this powerful breath, you can also help to co-create reality—you can intervene in the design, manifestation, and projection of what is happening around you.

According to Hindu tradition, the universe's very breath, that exhalation, sigh, or puff, possesses a sound. This vibration is what we know today as the sacred sound "Om."

Hindu scriptures further tell us that one day, after a vast expanse of time, the divine will inhale once more, symbolically swallowing all existence.

We will all return home, to the original energy!

Similarly, the Judeo-Christian concept of creation emphasizes the "word" as a divine exhalation. This notion is reinforced in Genesis, where vocal vibration (or the word) is attributed with creative power. This biblical clue suggests that the universe continues to be created, to expand, and to be revealed through the language of creation itself.

In the Basque spiritual tradition, it is said that when something is not named, it does not exist. Thus, for the trees to be born, they had to be named—this is an oak, this is a birch, this is a chestnut. The Basque gods had to name the animals so that they could emerge, and likewise, they named the lakes and rivers so that they would appear. Like the Judeo-Christian creation rite, all creation begins from vibration—therefore, with this preamble, it will be easier for us to understand that the universe is creating matter, forms, colors, all from vibrations arranged and rearranged in different ways.

Animals, water, light, and all living and inanimate beings are also encompassed by the immense play of creative energy.

This game draws you in and engulfs you completely. So much so that if you momentarily forget you're playing, you could easily fall into the wrong square—the game itself can devour you, ensnare you, and consume you.

Consider the example of a dedicated soccer fan. Imagine this individual engrossed in the game, captivated by the movements of the players, so immersed in the match that nothing else exists for them. Victory ignites an explosion of euphoria, enthusiasm, joy, and happiness. Conversely, defeat plunges them into despair and anger, obscuring the game's inherent triviality—it is just a game, not real life. But if the metaphor is not understood, they can end up bringing the drama of the game into real life, harming those around them due to an incident that occurred during the broadcast of a soccer match hundreds of miles away.

In the game of the ego, there are those who attain celebrity status, masquerading as masters, guides, or counselors. Yet, what lies beneath these carefully crafted personas? Ultimately, it is nothing more than a disguise. The ego, in its essence, is but another piece on the game board, a player in the realm of illusion. Therefore, it is crucial to distinguish between the game, or utopia of a fulfilled existence, and the totality of life itself.

On the other hand, in every game there are always two types of participants, always in contrast—those who enjoy themselves and those who don't, those who follow the rules and those who break them, those who know how to play and those who cheat. In the game of creative energy as depicted by the Hindus, the same holds true, and its players are called *līlā*, which has a meaning close to "to play/have fun."

Līlā (in Sanskrit) is a manifestation of the creative energy's loving eruption, giving rise to beings who engage in a cosmic game. Līlā involves two types of participants: those who are aware of the game's nature and those who are not. Those who are unaware of the game's true nature are often caught up in the illusion that the game is reality itself. They may perceive life as a meaningless struggle. Those who recognize the game's nature, understand that the game is a game and that life is life.

To illustrate this often-confusing spectrum for seekers of new truths, consider this real-life anecdote.

Emiliano Zapata, a prominent figure in the Mexican Revolution, was a peasant and military leader who championed the cause of Indigenous people and agricultural workers. As expected, those most affected by the injustices he sought to address became his ardent supporters. Zapata was easily recognizable by his imposing stature, wide-brimmed hat, and prominent mustache. It is said that after achieving victories in several of his campaigns, he arrived in the nation's capital accompanied by his army of peasants and officers, who were also of humble origins. Upon entering Mexico City, the Zapatista forces were welcomed with a theater performance organized by the city's residents. However, it is likely that none of the troops had ever had the opportunity to attend such a presentation before.

The troops arrived at their designated venue, the Esperanza Iris Theater, a renowned establishment that still stands today. Officers and soldiers alike filled the seats in the theater, and the performance began. The commotion in the story arose from a particularly intense scene where an actress is mistreated and shaken by another actor.

As part of the script, the struggle continued as the seemingly distressed damsel in peril cried out desperately, "Let me go! Let me go!" Abruptly, one of Zapata's soldiers stood up from his seat and sternly addressed the actor, "Didn't you hear? Let her go!"

The actor ignored the soldier's instruction, as he knew that, as dictated by the laws of show business, "the show must go on." The dialogue continued, and with it, his performance.

The soldier, visibly affected by what he was witnessing, and believing the scene was real, stood up again from his seat and repeated the order, "Let her go!" The play did not stop. Then the officer, extremely indignant at the defiance and believing he was fulfilling his duty to save the aggrieved woman, drew his pistol and shot the actor, killing him instantly.

This story, though deeply tragic, is also profoundly instructive. It serves as a stark reminder of the consequences of failing to recognize ourselves as spectators in the grand spectacle of creation. When we succumb to this oversight, we mistakenly perceive the characters in this play as real, when, in reality, they are merely actors playing their roles in our lives. This error, one we commit countless times, strips us of our ability to transcend the illusion and ensnares us within its confines.

Is succumbing to the latest smartphone, embracing fleeting fashion trends, or conforming to ever-changing beauty standards merely trivial? A closer look at collective behavior suggests a deeper entanglement in illusions, from which escape proves challenging.

Observe how many people who achieve a high rank, an important position, or a comfortable socioeconomic level have lost themselves by believing that they are their position, their economic level, or their rank—they get lost in the game without differentiating the character from the person. Look at the people who are fortunate enough to have an incredible house—when there is any threat of losing their property, they go crazy, fall into depression, and in unfortunate cases commit suicide because they do not understand that property is part of the props of the play and not the essential reality of the person. If we stop to see how many women and men lose their minds because they are running out of youth, freshness, or beauty, we will notice that these people end up attacking their own bodies by committing atrocities or undergoing surgery to the point of being disfigured, all in an attempt to recover an illusory image.

Beyond my skin, the game is tougher.

Hindu proverb

Upon venturing into the world, the game of reality becomes even more enticing, more dazzling, akin to a grand carnival. We all don our masks and step out, pretending to be something we are not to partake in the spectacle.

The astute Hindus, with their keen discernment, often remark upon this phenomenon, saying, "If I stray too far from myself, immersing myself in the carnival's revelry, I lose sight of my true self."

We are all participants in this universal carnival, whether it unfolds on the vibrant streets of Veracruz, the masked revelry of Venice, or any other form of distraction. This spectacle might manifest as a night out, a pursuit of material possessions, a relentless quest for physical perfection, or a desperate climb to spiritual or egoic supremacy. Such carnivals are deeply ingrained in our daily existence.

Do you recognize these patterns? Consider the pressures of school choices, the anxieties of social circles, the complexities of friendship, or the endless quest for the ideal vacation.

These carnivals, both grand and mundane, beckon us to participate. Whether willingly or unwittingly, we often find ourselves dancing to their rhythm. Yet, it's crucial to remember that these are merely diversions from our true selves.

Yes, the deeper we delve into this game, the further we risk losing ourselves.

The Hindu teaching offers a profound insight: "To avoid being ensnared by the world's game, I must turn inward—the deeper I go within, the less likely I am to lose myself in the external."

As clear as water, the more you venture into the world and disconnect from yourself, the greater the risk of getting caught up in illusion. But if you leave a trail of breadcrumbs, like Hansel and Gretel, you will always be able to navigate the game confidently and freely.

By learning to embrace your inner self—a gift I hope to share—you gain the freedom to fully engage in life's experiences. Enjoy the thrill, the laughter, and the playful spirit of life. Just remember—don't become consumed by the carnival.

How should you start applying this to your personal story? By consciously telling yourself: I am not the position they are giving me, I am not the money I have in the bank, I am not the car I drive, I am not the body I inhabit, I am not just a mother, I am not my job, I am not just a partner. . . . Embrace the role, embody it, and journey through it fully. However, remember, you are not defined by that role. It's a performance, a way of being you've chosen to explore. But when the time comes, shed the role gracefully, without drama or regrets. With awareness, you'll recognize that the game of creation is ever-changing. Sooner or later, the course will shift, and ultimately, the journey will lead you back to your authentic self.

This journey is twofold—an outward journey and an inward journey. This is why balance, walking the middle path, and following the focal point are essential to avoid getting lost. Go out, enjoy the world, have fun, but don't forget that after playing out there you have to come back to your inner self, to your truth.

Where is the line between play and reality? At what point does the game become a prison? The answer is simple—when you give more importance to the role and give it the authority to control your life through things like alcohol, drugs, sex, money, beauty, weight, muscles, intelligence, wisdom, spirituality, yoga, ego, power, and so on.

Do you recognize yourself in any of those prisons? Because if you can't stop and release awareness of the game, then you've been devoured.

Even if it seems like an exaggeration, when someone claims total obsession with an activity and professes an inability or unwillingness to stop, no matter how seemingly positive the habit (aerobic exercise, beauty routines, weight control, work meetings, reading), it becomes a sign of being trapped in the game.

Once we understand the nature of the game and the dangers of not knowing how to play it, the best thing to do is to emulate the great līlā and be able to step out and return to our essence, our soul, our truth.

The game is so cunning, it doesn't just trap you in vices and perdition. It's not just alcohol, drugs, and sex that are its main players—it can also trap us in unhealthy eating habits, a twisted spiritual path, or a seemingly selfless quest to save others or the whole world. Always remember: the best way not to get lost in the game is to establish a thread that leads you back, and stay in a conscious state, remembering that much of what you experience is simply a mirage.

Those who have been to India have witnessed it—there are few cultures as ostentatious as the Hindu, with its awe-inspiring palaces, its exquisite textiles and adorned attire, its gleaming bracelets and pendants. India is a country where the finest jewelry in the world is sold. Yet, this opulent facade conceals another side of the country—one of profound renunciation. Here, some individuals subsist on prana (breath) alone, embracing abject poverty and living an ascetic existence in the mountains, owning nothing.

In India, both extremes found embodiment in the lives of great masters. Buddha, a prince surrounded by every conceivable luxury, one day embarked on a radical departure from worldly pursuits, embracing the opposite extreme of asceticism and renunciation. Through his experiences, he discovered that neither path led to true fulfillment. Thus, he charted a new course—the middle path.

I believe in the middle path as well, and I know it is not about renouncing the whole world or possessing all desires—I know there is a path where one can enjoy the world without being devoured by it.

How can I gauge my alignment with the center? One indicator is the degree of attachment to the world. For instance, consider someone who professes spirituality and detachment but then encounters the following situation:

"Hey, did you lose your *japa mala*, your prayer beads? Because I don't see you wearing it."

"Oh no! My japa mala! The Dalai Lama gave it to me . . . I can't lose it, it's the most sacred thing I have!"

Well, let me tell you, that's attachment. We find carnivals like this everywhere—even in subtle ways, we cling to the world.

Imagine you went on vacation and had a wonderful time at the beach, swimming among beautiful and friendly waves. But when it's time to go home, if you find yourself lamenting what you can no longer enjoy, instead of understanding that life must continue its daily course—this is because you remain oblivious to the concept of transformation. You are still not grounded in your reality and remain in the role of a swimmer. The same is true if you once had financial freedom, a successful professional life, and now you have less income due to problems at your company. If the taste of glory has faded and no one remembers your days of good fortune anymore, clinging to that glorious past will not do much good if you do not end up accepting with peace that life goes on.

We all have the crucial task of recognizing the game as just that—a game. To stop taking life so seriously and to understand that the people who hurt, wound, and harm us are all part of the game. But, you know, all your detractors are necessary for your learning—the people who harmed your life to some extent have a purpose within the grand plan. Just like the father who abandoned his children, like the woman who cheated on her husband, or like the boss who made an unjustified dismissal, every player has a part. Just as a generous benefactor propels us forward, so too do our challenges. Mastering this game unlocks life's full potential.

When we blur the lines between the game and truth, the game consumes us, transforming us into mice trapped within its confines. We become convinced that the sole purpose of existence lies in chasing cheese, the ultimate prize. Our lives become consumed by the pursuit of work, wealth, physical perfection, romantic relationships, parenthood, success, triumph, and victory. Ensnared in this game, we relentlessly chase an insatiable hunger for a nourishment that eludes our grasp, trapped within a labyrinth that, if left unrecognized, can stretch into infinity. However, if we can learn to distinguish between the game and truth, we can have fun and embrace the dance of reality, as it is called in shamanism.

It is an experience of great pleasure when we learn to enjoy and laugh at ourselves, and also to laugh at the game. We can learn to recognize that we do not have to renounce the world, because it is incredible and fun. We learn that we can enjoy the beautiful things this experience gives us, but at the same time remember, in every moment, every night, or at least once a day, that we are in a game and that we have to return to ourselves. That process of returning is pure consciousness; it is like going to a party or a vacation and having a great time, but then knowing we have to go home to enjoy something more authentic.

Let's expand on the vacation example. For a few weeks, you go to a new place and everything is bliss. Someone makes your bed, serves you breakfast, treats you like royalty. It's phenomenal. But then you have to go back home and take care of the housework, and you have to accept that it's neither good nor bad—it's just different, it's part of the game.

Vacations are undoubtedly enjoyable, offering opportunities for relaxation and amusement. However, they represent only a portion of life. Life itself encompasses the ordinary routines and simple pleasures that fill our days at home. The key question lies in finding balance: Can we experience the tranquility of completing everyday tasks with the same intensity as the joy of a luxurious vacation? Can a simple meal of bread and tea, savored in a peaceful atmosphere, bring us as much delight as a gourmet meal?

A fundamental principle for attaining spiritual consciousness lies in recognizing and understanding freedom. Freedom is nothing more than experiencing the game as a game and returning to one's essence as essence—it is knowing that what is important will always remain important.

Let's consider a more relatable example. Imagine you have a teenage son who comes to you one day and says, "I'm going to take drugs. Will you let me do drugs every day? I promise I'll stop and come back home later." How would you respond to such a request?

Similarly, if a drunk person asks you, "Can I borrow your car? It's really fast and I want to go for a drive." Would you lend it to them?

What do the teenager and the drunk person have in common? Besides a lot of glee, they both lack consciousness. To be conscious is to recognize that there are times when we are intoxicated and incapable of making decisions. In order to achieve this discernment between the game and the truth, we need to detoxify ourselves, enter a state of calm, clarity, and consciousness.

If you are not in that state, you will hardly be able to recognize the line that separates the game from the truth.

So, we must ask ourselves: How do we attain a state of higher consciousness? How do we come home? How do we recognize that we are too engrossed in the game and that it is time to take a step back?

The answer lies in silence, meditation, prayer, spirituality, Universal Laws, and—above all—your heart. I am confident that if you apply these teachings with an open mind and consistency, you will begin to discover the fine line that separates the game of authenticity from the reality of life.

I recommend you establish a reminder symbol to help you understand when you are leaving the game and returning to yourself, to the essential, to your home. When you leave your house, you understand that you are going out into the world to fulfill your work and the functions that society demands of you, but you can remind yourself through a simple act like taking off your shoes, lighting incense, diffusing essential oil, or lighting a candle that you are back home, that you are no longer the boss or the public figure but simply you, with the people you love most, in the plainness and beauty of your daily life.

I once had the opportunity to accompany a great teacher and very dear friend of mine named Karen. A very special person with a lot of influence, a true rockstar. I happened to be in New York with her, where we went to several restaurants. She exuded an aura of glamour unlike anything I had ever witnessed, and we always got the best tables. It was as if I were walking alongside a Hollywood celebrity. However, upon returning to her apartment in an affluent New York neighborhood, a remarkable transformation took place as soon as we crossed the threshold. A profound inner shift, reflected in her physical demeanor, washed over her. She retreated, donned a lovely robe, and removed her wig. Engaging in a personal ritual, she softly uttered to herself, "I'm back, Karen."

I wholeheartedly embrace the practice of acknowledging our return home with a simple, "I'm back." Whether it's "Miguel Ángel, I'm back" or "Mónica, we're back," this declaration transforms daily life. It's a moment to shed our public personas and embrace our private selves. Instead of "the director's wife," we become "a mortal being going to bed." Instead of "the judge of the Supreme Court," we become "an ordinary man getting dressed."

This constant and conscious symbolic act is a gift to the soul. We must also say "I'm back" on terrible, difficult days—days that shake us up, and days when we realize we can't take any more pain.

Difficult moments are also part of the game, and when we acknowledge that we're back, we're telling ourselves, "We're home—the game and its complex circumstances are over." The fictional idea that everything falls apart has to stop, because what's essential doesn't fall apart. Nothing authentic and true can be destroyed. It's the game that breaks. It's the surface that's damaged in the soul. Your Higher Self remains intact.

Just as a color spectrum encompasses a range of hues, so too does the game of life present a diverse array of elements. At one end lies the radiant brilliance of white, while at the opposite extreme resides the somber depth of black.

Dark games make you forget there is light. If you're distracted or don't have strong awareness, you'll get lost in these games, forgetting the light within you. You'll also forget the journey back to your essence and become sadly immersed in the darkness, the trap, the game's darkest and heaviest part.

It's essential to remember that not everything you experience with your senses is real or important. The key is to maintain your awareness, recognize your inner light, return to your self again and again, spend as much time as possible in solitude, and learn to enjoy vacations while also appreciating the peaceful everyday life of your home.

Just as tiny sparks rise from a fire,
so too do all the worlds, all the gods,
and all beings arise from this Ātman.

Bṛihadāraṇyaka Upanishad

Universal Law I

Principle of Oneness

There is a great universal consequence, and everything that exists is a manifestation of this consciousness.

Imagine a net as large and flexible as those cast by fishermen into the sea. You are standing nearby, like a witness, watching the moment the net rises, twirls in the air, and spreads out like a large skirt over the surface of the sea. It is a beautiful spectacle.

Now imagine that you are the fisherman. You have sailed far out to sea well before sunrise. You have commitments to fulfill, and despite the accumulated fatigue of so many days of work, you exert great effort, heaving the weighty net with both arms, its expanse mirroring the vastness of your hope for a bountiful catch.

Imagine now you are a fish, swimming as usual, in pursuit of sustenance, when suddenly, an intricately woven, alien cloud—the net—descends upon you, rendering you immobile. Now picture yourself as a somewhat disoriented fish, drifting along oblivious, unaware that you're ensnared in a net, only noticing the sudden presence of other fish here and there, huddled beside you as an inexplicable tug hoists you toward the surface.

What if, instead of being a fish, you are a microscopic plankton particle, and the net falls on you? Surely you would not be able to comprehend the immensity of that woven structure, and a single strand of it would seem like a giant load beam that has fallen on you.

What if you were an artist standing on a cliff, watching the fisherman's boat from afar? Perhaps you would just see a human figure throwing something out of the boat. The perspective you would have on this event would surely be very different due to the distance. You would see a kind of cape falling into the water and you might think it would be a beautiful scene to capture in a painting.

The nature of the net varies depending on the individual and their level of consciousness.

Some people are like the fisherman, others are like the alert fish, still others are like the unaware fish. Some are like the plankton, and some others are like the artist.

Increased consciousness accelerates our awareness of the approaching net. Unconscious fish are swept away, unaware of their predicament. More alert fish can react. Fishermen understand the net's purpose. Artists perceive the event from a different vantage point. Our perspective is shaped by our consciousness and awareness.

Our co-creative role begins here, as continuers of creation. If the net is cast, and you are part of the group that is caught in it, this does not mean you are doomed to the same fate as everyone else.

Instead, as you become more conscious of the net, gain more experience, and develop a broader vision, you will be able to choose different ways of coexisting with it. You could decide to position yourself in the least tense or constricted part. You could have a certain margin of maneuver, or be completely trapped in the center. In this way the net can be fun, instructive, interesting—or a process of total suffering. This will mostly depend on your level of consciousness.

Remember that we are all within a Great Divine Net, all linked by a network of energies that function like the threads of a net, only there are many different ways to perceive the presence of it. This is the Principle of Oneness, the first Universal Law with which we will work. Are you ready now?

Oneness is not the same as unity—oneness goes much further. It is the interconnection between all the parts that make up the whole.

The Principle of Oneness tells us there is a vast universal consciousness and everything that exists is a manifestation of that consciousness. Everything we perceive is actually distinct vibrations of a single focal point, different elements of a single essence. This great consciousness connects us all, and maintains a balance and higher order for all the parts that make it up.

LEVELS OF CONSCIOUSNESS

When we speak of spirituality, we refer to a different perspective on reality, or "levels of consciousness." These levels are what will determine our reading, our understanding, our comprehension, and the actions we generate in response to what happens to us. Referring back to the parable of the net, the artist perceives and is aware, from his height, of a very different reality than that of the fish, who is subjected to and forced to suffer the effects of its reality.

I recall an incident involving a man who suffered a lateral paralysis. His wife requested my presence at their home. Upon my arrival, I found the couple's three children present, one of whom was deeply angered by his father's illness. He exclaimed, "How the hell are we going to pay for the hospital? How irresponsible of him to choose cerebral palsy or a neuronal outburst when we have no money!" But the second son's behavior caught my attention. He followed closely behind his mother, holding a cup while repeatedly asking, "Mommy, would you like some coffee? Mommy, would you like some coffee?" His mind seemed fixated on that single question. The youngest, their daughter, threw a tantrum because her mother had pulled her away from a gathering with her friends just when she was having the most fun. I stood there observing, thinking to myself, *The universe is filled with beings operating at different levels of consciousness.* The daughter resentful toward her mother for interrupting her nail painting, one son fixated on his mother to an obsessive degree, and the other enraged at his father for falling ill. What a dilemma!

This was like a snapshot of life. What part of the movie are we seeing? What are we recognizing from the play? What are we perceiving from the Grand Design? What do we understand about what is happening to us? Usually, we only see the part that interests us, but this does not exempt us from the great process of the planetary network or the Principle of Oneness.

Consciousness levels fluctuate constantly. While we may attain a level-three consciousness, a bad day could push us back to level two. Recognizing this variability is crucial. By cultivating sustained high-level consciousness, we can enhance our overall life experience. Therefore, higher consciousness leads to a good life.

Achieving this requires reading, meditating, taking courses, attending classes, self-reflection, practicing mindfulness, and promoting self-awareness.

A book like the one you hold in your hands can help raise your level of consciousness. Anyone who achieves excellence in any endeavor has gone through a process. Each person must dedicate time, attention, and effort to the things they want to see grow in their life. Therefore, it is important to recognize that consciousness is a process, and that it can be exercised. As much as possible, make your consciousness a necessary tool for your evolution.

It would be great if we could stop seeing spirituality as just a hobby and instead commit to working every day toward a better version of ourselves. This means abandoning those everyday excuses where we look at the path of growth as entertainment, and instead taking responsibility and bringing spirituality into all possible areas of our lives.

The Principle of Oneness reminds us that we are part of a vast network that connects everything, that each element is crucial for the functioning of the whole, and that everything that happens has an order, a balance, an equilibrium, and a higher harmony. If we learn to recognize this network, then we can live in harmony and with a high level of consciousness, achieving peace, trusting that the Higher Power governs our lives.

THE ONGOING NATURE OF CREATION

We exist within an ongoing creation, not a finished one. You yourself are unfinished, and even death doesn't mark completion. Your life's work, your relationships—as parent or child—none of it truly ends. If we are indeed part of a grand source, a greater whole, then we hold the power to influence it.

Shamanic tradition holds a creation myth featuring a very special being—the Great Spider Grandmother. One of three essential beings born from the Divine's heart, the Spider Grandmother fulfills a crucial role. With her web, she weaves connections between everything being created. These fine threads bind parents and children, spouses in love, couples. They also connect a town and its inhabitants, a businessman and his venture, and a poet with his poetry.

This woven thread extends not only from a tree to its descendants but also to the descendants of a species, a culture, or a family.

These invisible threads, though unseen, are ever-present—the narrative threads of a story that continually grows, expands, and flourishes.

Spider Grandmother serves as a poignant reminder that the threads of creation are intricately interwoven, connecting every experience, action, and dream within a vast and boundless network.

This is how the Principle of Oneness operates. When a mother senses her child's vibration, she perceives it swiftly and intensely, as something deeply felt, because her own energy shares a close affinity with her child's, despite the physical separation.

This is also why that feeling of special connection with those closest to us permeates us so strongly when they are happy or sad, feel alone, or need something from us.

Some things feel closer to us, while others feel more distant. According to shamanic beliefs, this has to do with the distance and thickness of the thread spun by the Great Spider Grandmother. We have a greater sense of connection and belonging with certain events, experiences, or people, and this is all related to the strength of the thread that binds us to them.

In shamanism, it is even believed that humans possess the ability to sever the threads of the Spider Grandmother's web and reweave them. We can mend those threads of connection, those threads that may have weakened and frayed at some point.

One example of how the Great Spider Grandmother's threads work is conception. When a couple asks for a baby, they are asking for a thread. The time it takes for that thread to reach the great mother, the great source, and be answered, is the time it takes for pregnancy to manifest. If it sometimes takes two or three years, or if it is a pregnancy that occurs at the first encounter, it is partly influenced by the great consciousness that knows it is the time for that soul to come into the world, that it is the time for the parents to give birth. Our consciousness of oneness varies depending on our perspective, our knowledge, and our wisdom.

Imagine a garden with a single flower. Inside its petals lives a tiny bug. For this inhabitant, the flower is its entire world—both sky and earth are contained within its boundaries. The flower is the bug's entire reality. For a bird, however, the flower is just one among many in the garden. Its world is far vaster than the bug's confined world within the flower. But, for a person strolling through the garden, the bird, the flower, and the bug are all interconnected pieces. The bird belongs to the garden, the flower adorns the garden, and the bug resides within the flower. Finally, if someone observes the garden from a great height, flying overhead, they might see a man in the garden and think the man is also part of the garden.

Therefore, as we become more conscious, we gain a clearer understanding of the Principle of Oneness. Our level of spiritual awareness determines the scope of our perceived oneness. At a lower, more fundamental level of consciousness, we believe we are connected only to people and things we love—our children, parents, partners, home, and possessions. However, as we progress, we realize we are also linked to a broader group of people, an extended family, friends, teachers, and those who touch our lives and leave an indelible mark.

And if we elevate our consciousness even further, we perceive our connection to the planet, to an elephant, and that elephant's connection to a star in the sky, which in turn is linked to the cosmic dust traveling between galaxies. Oneness transcends the notion of unified individuals to encompass planetary beings, spiritual beings, enlightened beings, and ultimately, the understanding that we are all part of the Great Whole.

When we understand that beings are connected to cosmic planes, when we understand it is not just about our planet but about the totality of creation, and that we are capable of discovering we are part of a divine consciousness that continues to expand, we form a thought that has not been completed. We understand we are a creation in motion and that we can modify our reality, our destiny, and ourselves. Then we have reached a good level of consciousness, of oneness.

Since creation is ongoing, we become co-creators of our reality. Imagine a painting. If it were finished, varnished and sealed, no further brushstrokes could be added. However, when a painting is in progress, its fresh canvas welcomes additional color.

The wonderful part that concerns us is that our life is still being painted, and that is a great gift. That is why free will exists.

We are not condemned to a preordained narrative—we are co-creators of the story we inhabit. Grasping this concept from a conscious perspective will empower us to influence a small or a grand narrative, transcending the limitations of a personal human story of seventy, eighty, or ninety years.

Some time ago, I took an angel channeling course where I learned that angels perceive us, humans, as tiny pixels. Our limited vision is akin to a bug trapped inside a flower. We perceive reality in a pixelated manner, resulting in a distorted appreciation of our surroundings. To observe the complete and defined image, we need to step back and gain perspective. The more distance we create, the clearer the image becomes.

Sometimes we complain about going through a bad time, a period of crisis. We have thoughts like, "Life is very unfair and doesn't care about me," and we go on, in victim mode, "I am a martyr of Calvary." Then, the angels respond, "You are only seeing a small part of the movie." And we refute by saying, "Yes, but that little part is my whole reality." And the angels wisely say, "No, that little part is not your whole reality. It is the portion of reality you are able to perceive."

It is similar to what happens with art in general, and with some paintings in particular. There is a perfect distance to appreciate the painting. If you get too close you won't understand the context, but if you move too far away you'll lose it too. That is why it is necessary to wait for moments of mental clarity and inner peace to be able to perceive what is happening to you in its correct dimension and with its clear messages. Life has a perfection we can only appreciate when we are able to place ourselves in the perfect energy level.

I close this chapter with a question that can bring you great clarity if you learn to observe within yourself:

How does what happens outside somehow reside within me?

Get used to seeing with new eyes. Every time you complain, every time you argue, every time something makes you angry, every time something disgusts you, ask yourself: How does what happens outside connect to something that is happening inside me? You must cultivate the ability to reflect on external events as internal reflections. Although it may seem a bit distant, if you are a good observer, you will find how the outside world is a reflection of what is happening inside you.

Life's challenges present unique messages to each individual. Financial ruin holds distinct significance for everyone who experiences it. Similarly, a terminal illness carries personalized meaning and information for each person affected. When we understand that the outside world only activates things that were already inside, and later understand that the world inside co-creates the world outside, we can affirm our participation in universal interconnectedness.

Affirmations for the Principle of Oneness

Drawing on the Principle of Oneness, I offer three affirmations. These powerful statements carry an energetic charge, and will help you vibrate at a frequency that shapes your reality. You can engage with them in various ways—by working on them, internalizing them, or simply becoming aware of their message. Integrate them into your life, and watch them manifest.

- *I am pure potentiality that, in consciousness, is transformed into generation.*

The purpose of this affirmation is to show all your light, all your strength. If you focus on it, you can generate a lot of wonderful events around you.

- *I am part of the whole.*

This means that, even if you can't see it, everything is perfectly woven together. We are part of an invisible chain, and what is happening to you is just a small fragment of a great plan you may not be able to understand.

- *Everything ebbs and flows for my highest good.*

This acknowledges that in this Great Web everything is moving toward a single direction, in an evolutionary sense, and this grand plan encourages authenticity, well-being, cooperation, and inner peace for each of us.

You are the co-creator of everything in your reality through your vibrations.

Gordana Biernat

Universal Law II

Principle of Generation

The seeds I sow within me bear fruit in my external reality.

Aniline is a highly concentrated substance. A few grams of aniline dropped into a large tank of water will gradually spread its color throughout the transparency of the water, dyeing it completely. A pinch of this pigment is capable of coloring the entire container. A small amount of this substance can permeate everything around it.

Spiritually speaking, some people are like water, while others are like aniline—we have the power to influence the entirety of what contains us. We have the capacity to imbue our lives with what we carry in our hearts.

We are all participants in the grand game of life, but we also actively contribute to its unfolding. Remember, beyond mere spectators, we are co-creators shaping its course. Given our capacity to influence this grand stage, consider these questions: How can you make it change? What impact can I make? How far-reaching is my influence within this great game?

You may wonder: How does someone possess such tremendous strength and the ability to influence external reality? How can someone declare, "I choose to flow with the games and change my destiny"? And, conversely, how can some live condemned to submit, and resign themselves to the flow of games created by someone else?

The answer is very clear—the more resonance affinity I have with the game, the more parts of it will play in my favor. When many choose to vibrate at the same frequency, when they come together, that frequency amplifies and it becomes easier for those people to achieve their purpose. The stronger the sum of the intentions and purposes of those who pursue the same goal, the greater their capacity to powerfully influence and generate reality.

By applying the phrase "greatest universal good," you harness the immense energy of the greater good and integrate it into your purpose. Similarly, by setting the intention of "seeking the greater good," it will be woven into the fabric of your objective. The more you incorporate the well-being of many into your driving force, the more your intention will be amplified.

A common mistake when working with the Principle of Generation is focusing solely on personal gain. Imagine yourself as a minuscule flea in a vast universe. If you declare, "I want this for myself," the universe might respond, "Perhaps, but only on a flea-sized scale." However, if you, the flea, could somehow influence a horse to desire the same thing, your influence would amplify dramatically. Together, with the horse's collaboration, your desires could be realized on a grander, more impactful level. This illustrates the powerful connection between the Principle of Generation and our ability to shape reality.

The pursuit of the greater good is the fundamental purpose of the Principle of Generation, and therefore it cannot be understood without first comprehending the Principle of Oneness. I must ensure that what I generate benefits humanity, and that it interacts and flows positively. And I must be very clear that the more energy I manage to put into my intentions, the easier it will be for what I want to happen to manifest.

This is the Principle of Generation. We are both creation and creator. The energy that composes us is the same energy that composes all things. At a chemical level, the universe consists of the same elements in varying proportions. The universe's raw material is uniform—we are stardust, and many life forms on Earth share a composition of carbon, hydrogen, oxygen, and nitrogen. Each of these elements is rooted in a deeper essence—vibration, the primordial "Om" from which all life originates.

Now, I want to highlight two fundamental aspects of the Principle of Generation. Understanding these aspects is essential; internalizing and integrating them into your life is paramount for manifesting your desires:

1. We are creation and we are creator. The energy we are made of is the same energy that all things are made of.
2. With consciousness, attention, and intention, you can encode and recreate the essence of anything. By understanding the fundamental components of matter, you can arrange and rearrange them to manifest your desires and aspirations.

Understand that a single raw material can be transformed into countless possibilities. When you discover this main component, you can create whatever you want.

When a musician grasps the essence of music, you can give them an Afghan drum, a bongo, or an African drum and with any of them, the musician can create music. Their proficiency stems from understanding music's composition and its underlying principles. With a deep knowledge of the musical code—percussion, rhythm, melody, and harmony—they can create a beautiful musical experience with any type of instrument.

We are called to be musicians of the spirit, to understand the codes of energy and vibration. If we understand this fundamental structure of the game, and are able to discover that the game is essentially energy and vibration, then we can add them together and influence the final outcome.

THE CODE OF GENERATION

I'd like to share a golden rule with you, a fundamental teaching that states, "Generation can occur, in part, through awareness of the code, attention to vibration, and openness to the miraculous, recognizing that we and all things are essentially energy."

Let's break down these components.

What is the code called? What is code awareness?

The code is energy and vibration. The vibration we emit opens up the possibility of generating what we choose in the game board.

Code awareness is paying attention to what we are constantly emitting.

The Principle of Generation can be summarized in a single phrase: "If it happens within me, it happens on my path."

I'd like to share a short story about the power of this phrase and the importance of inner and outer alignment. In 2017, my students and I visited an extraordinarily beautiful place, a magical and very special site called Roraima, a mountain nestled in the interior of Venezuela, in a region known as La Gran Sabana. The original inhabitants gave it this name, which means "mother of all waters." It's a spectacular place, but very difficult to access. Getting to the starting point is already tough, then you have to walk for at least three days—without any means of transportation except your feet—covering great distances, battling mosquitoes, and crossing rivers, but always supported by Indigenous guides from the *Pemón* tribe, who work as porters. These guides carry the entire camp—the kitchen, the food, the tents, and all the supplies used on the trip, including the bathroom.

After three days of hiking under a scorching sun, we reached the base of a colossal mountain. Standing there, taking in its towering height, was an awe-inspiring experience. We dedicated an entire day to climbing it.

Our families and friends were deeply confused by our decision to travel to Venezuela. The country was in the midst of a crisis, and we were met with questions like, "Why would you go to a country that's so dangerous and complex, especially in the midst of such difficult political and social unrest?"

Amidst this external chaos, we decided to turn our attention inward. Together, we created a phrase of profound resonance and great power: "If there is peace within me, there will be peace on my path." We resolved to embark on our journey to Venezuela with inner peace, opening ourselves up from a deep place to allow everything to flow in the best possible, most harmonious way. Despite the challenging circumstances, our inner vibration and energy did their work—the paths always opened up smoothly and peacefully.

We took a plane to Caracas and then a bus to a city called Puerto Ordaz. From there we changed transportation again and reached the base camp after hiking for three days, followed by one day of ascent. We enjoyed four or five days on top of Roraima and then descended, also on a very strenuous hike.

To return to the Venezuelan capital from Puerto Ordaz, we had a serious conflict with the airlines, as there were no planes taking off. At that time, Venezuela only had two aircraft to cover all routes. But we—despite the refusals and how impossible it seemed—remained with that intention, vibrating and affirming: "If there is peace within me, there will be peace on my path."

At one point, it evolved into a slightly different phrase: "If it happens within me, it will happen on my path." Consequently, when our flight was canceled, we chose meditation over chaos. Amidst the airport's turmoil, we maintained a meditative state, repeating the mantra "Let's unlock the miracle."

Despite being told it was impossible, we persevered, pulsating, transmitting, and trusting that things would work out for the best. While others gave up and left the airport due to the cancellation, we remained, steadfast in our belief—trusting, trusting, trusting.

In a peculiar turn of events, many hours later—perhaps six or seven—we spotted a plane that had arrived significantly delayed. And from that magical moment on, those who shared this experience (incredible beings) would say to each other, "If there is peace within me, there will be peace on my path," or "If it happens within me, it will happen on my path," with fond memories of our adventure.

Therefore, we can understand that while the Principle of

Oneness makes you responsible and aware of everything around you and how everything is interconnected, the Principle of Generation makes you the architect and co-creator of what you want to surround yourself with.

REFLECTING ON YOUR SURROUNDINGS

Take some time for self-reflection and ask yourself: What is happening in your surroundings? What are the people closest to you complaining about? In what kind of world, in what kind of life, do you live? At what point in your personal history are you? At what stage of your evolutionary cycle are you right now? What stories do you tell yourself in your head?

Everything that surrounds you, although it may sound a bit harsh, is part of what you have co-created, of how you have employed the Principle of Generation. And while not everything is 100 percent your responsibility, you must start by understanding that you have influenced the reality that surrounds you, and what you are going through.

The house you inhabit, the space you occupy—whether stifling, overwhelming, beautiful, clean, dirty, open, spacious, or healthy—is your creation. If your home is a cherished haven, well-lit, pleasant, and harmonious, congratulations! You've manifested it.

Conversely, if your home consists of cramped, malodorous rooms, plagued by poor lighting and a noisy neighbor, you must acknowledge your partial role in generating this.

And if you imagine that the house is communicating with you and realize your surroundings are reflections of your inner world, you can undergo a transformation. This understanding aligns with the Principle of Generation.

If you are a neurotic person who relies on four Valium a day to maintain composure and is reluctant to reduce medication, preferring instead a "peaceful and serene" demeanor as if you were a Hindu yogi, you have a problem ahead of you. Because it is not just about looking like a yogi. Genuine embodiment requires internal vibration, heartfelt sensation, and a pulsating sense of peace emanating from the heart. Only then will your external reality mirror the tranquility cultivated within.

It's not about external affirmations or projections of energy; it is, in reality, about *generating*. If you want to generate love, generate it in yourself. If you want to generate abundance, generate it in yourself. If you want to generate peace, generate it in yourself.

Understanding the Principle of Oneness serves as a platform for comprehending and applying the Principle of Generation. This is because these two principles are interconnected—only one who recognizes themselves deeply and embraces their part in the whole can understand they are capable of influencing that whole by generating the correct vibration, energy, and consciousness within.

Therefore, according to the Principle of Generation, if I want to repair something outside, I must first do so within, recognizing that I am the focal point from which everything arises. I am a central generator of my reality. What lives within me produces or influences what surrounds me.

WHAT ARE YOU EMITTING?

We are generators. Human beings possess both pulsating and magnetic energy, meaning we are both receptive and emissive. When we understand that we receive information from life but also emit information to life, we stop victimizing ourselves. People in the victim role perceive themselves as passive recipients of life's offerings, shaping their actions and reactions accordingly.

However, when we shift our paradigm and realize we also emit energetic vibrations to life, we choose to leave behind the victim mentality and take an active role. We understand that we are responsible or co-responsible for what has happened to us, so we speak to the universe with our hearts to ask for what we truly want to experience.

The idea of understanding the human being as a generator is formidable because, in this way, we can understand that what one emits, what one pulsates, and the energy charges one produces, whether consciously or unconsciously, are constantly emitting packets of information to reality. This happens constantly and continuously. All the time, your thoughts, emotions, feelings, ideas, and stories are emitting energy waves outward, which reality takes and reflects back to you.

Imagine being a radio that is turned on twenty-four hours a day, seven days a week, 365 days a year, broadcasting continuously. The vibration you emit comes in the form of constant and continuous packets of information—but not always consciously. To my shamanism students, I teach the word "irradiation." When a body emits waves of energy in all directions, and expands these waves around it, it is said to be radiating. It is like a sun from which rays of light and heat emanate.

It is very important to constantly ask yourself: What am I radiating right now? Am I emitting gratitude? Am I emitting peace? Am I emitting conflict? What I emit charges the information field—the weaker my emanation, the longer it takes to charge or add energy to it so what I am generating manifests.

Some individuals possess a powerful emanation. If they proclaim, for example, "I want a fight," with remarkable swiftness, they manifest it. This conflict they externalized with such speed is not solely the product of their desire but also stems from the information their field is constantly emitting regarding their persistent request. It's as if they're preparing themselves for reality, the so-called "software of the universe," programming themselves with the instruction "fight, fight, fight." Thus, when the command is given, they deploy this programming and it manifests in their lives.

Others excel at manifesting illness or lack, but these manifestations are unconscious. In such cases, it's not the Principle of Generation at play but rather a reactive manifestation. Reactive manifestation is what occurs without conscious effort. In other words, the person is acting without making a choice. This often happens to people who are constantly complaining, anxious, or argumentative, or to those who are always worried about running out of money.

When I talk about the Principle of Generation, I am referring to proactive action. I choose to emit what I am emitting. For example, a woman who is looking for a partner might say, "I'm going to go out and meet someone new today." And she goes out and finds a potential partner. She attracts them because that energy is there, strongly condensed, and she can emit it.

It's crucial to frequently ask yourself, "What am I consistently emitting into the universe?" Your emissions charge and program your information field. By radiating desires for delicious food, gifts, affection, peace, love, and pampering, you infuse the universe with this energy, which can manifest when needed. The universe responds to your inner energy. Imagine a universal information field where someone declares, "I deserve a raise!" This charged declaration attracts the desired outcome. Conversely, a lack of such energy can hinder manifestation. A profound aspect of the Principle of

Generation is the direct correlation between manifestation ability and energetic output.

We all know remarkable individuals who seem to manifest their desires with ease. They declare, "I want a partner," and voilà, a partner appears. They say, "I want a chocolate cake," and presto, a chocolate cake materializes.

To those observing from the outside, it might seem inexplicable, extraordinary, or perhaps a matter of luck. However, in reality, these individuals have spent considerable time generating energy through a thought, an emotion, or an affirmation. For instance, they might repeat, "Everything I desire manifests quickly." When they devote time and attention to this thought or affirmation, they gradually build it into a part of their reality. When the object of their desire finally appears, they are ready to embrace it.

It's not an instantaneous feat. It requires a high level of vibrational and energetic preparation before it can simply coalesce and manifest. Similar to a cake when it's ready to come out of the oven—it took some time to bake, and the person who baked it bought the ingredients long before the cake was ready.

Remember that you are the generator of both conflict and peace, of change or stagnation, of things moving forward, flowing, and happening. Become aware of this and your life will change.

CREATING THE FOUNDATION FOR GENERATION

To be in a position of generation, you need to vibrate high, keep your energy clean, your mind clear, and your attention focused on the desire you want to achieve. You need to be consistent with what you are about to achieve. You cannot see abundance manifested if you are generating lack from within with doubts, fears, or selfish attitudes. You cannot ask for love to manifest in your life if you do not love yourself within your heart. You cannot ask for manifested health if you are constantly thinking about illness and afraid to live a life of fullness and complete health.

Therefore, you must know that the universe, in a structured way, receives your pulsations. But when you are emitting many pulsations at once, it will receive the strongest one. Basically, we emit four types of pulsations: mental, bodily, emotional, and spiritual. Which of the four will the universe listen to the most? Remember—it will be the one that has the most force of emanation, the one that has the most coherence with you, the one where you are most present, most attentive, and where your energy vibrates the highest.

Can different frequencies be emitted at the same time? The answer is yes. In fact, we do it most of the time. Perhaps your body and your voice say "I apologize," but your heart is saying "I'm furious with you." And maybe your voice says "Okay," but the energy that comes out of your voice is level two, and the energy of fury, which emerges from your heart, is level six. In this case, the universe will register the level two of the body, but will respond mostly to the level six energy of the emotion, because it is the one vibrating the strongest.

A fundamental idea I would like you to keep in mind is that we are a generating point. What I experience in myself is reflected in what surrounds me. If I want to correct something, I first correct it within myself. If I intend to release something, I first release it within myself. If I want to see something manifested, I first manifest it within myself as if it were a fact.

If your desire is to correct injustice in the world, start by correcting the injustice within you; if you want to correct the pain of women in the world, start by healing the feminine part within you.

If I feel separate from the whole, I am merely an observer of life's unfolding. However, when I grasp the Principles of Oneness and Generation, I recognize my role as a co-creator. The totality I inhabit is the same totality I can influence. This realization initiates a transformative journey of self-discovery, growth, and change.

I am sure that applying these laws will change your life positively.

Once the above is understood, paradoxical choices arise: Do I worry about the lack of money or do I focus on generating the appropriate vibration to attract money? Do I worry about illness and all the harm it can bring to my life, or do I focus on generating the vibration that brings me closer to health?

If you are just waiting for something external to happen to solve your problems, you are tied down. You will always depend on what is beyond your control. But if you recognize that you can be a proactive creator, you will cease to be a victim who laments what happens and become a true co-creator and generator of your reality.

Start generating within yourself now what you desire to see in the world. Abandon nonsense and excuses, and cultivate inner strength. Expand your consciousness to recognize the power to positively influence your circumstances. Similarly, cherish the beautiful aspects of your life to ensure their enduring presence.

Generate change from within, and you'll discover a transformative power. Like aniline, you'll color the world around you, manifesting previously unimaginable realities. Beyond the constraints of logic and material existence, you can reshape your experience. You're no longer merely a player in a predetermined game but a co-creator of its rules.

A powerful way to apply these laws is through small psychomagical acts. These practices heighten consciousness and amplify your vibrational impact within the līlā, the cosmic playing field.

Four Psychomagical Acts for the Principle of Generation

I'm going to give you four very everyday psychomagical acts you can do to be aware of what you need to emit to the world.

1. *Find a small ritual that brings you back to yourself each day, bringing you to conscious awareness. This could be something like applying oil to your skin before bed, or taking a few deep breaths and becoming aware that you are a being rather than a character in a play. Another option is to become aware that you are returning to your sanctuary when you cross the threshold of your home, leaving behind the material world and its forms so you can connect with your own creative essence.*

2. *Open the palms of your hands as if you were an antenna, and ask yourself: What am I radiating to the world right now? What am I emitting, what am I pulsating? What am I vibrating, and with what kind of emotions am I experiencing this present moment? You can do a little twist, as if adjusting your antenna, and then ask yourself: What do I want to emit? What do I want to pulsate at this moment or for this particular circumstance?*

3. *This is a very simple act: when washing your hands, feel the water removing everything you don't want to project, as if washing away negative thoughts and emotions along with the dirt. Let them go, let them fall away, and stay refreshed so you can project, vibrate, and generate the energy you truly desire in that moment.*

4. *Find a small symbol, something you can carry with you every day. It could be a bracelet, a ring, a watch, a colorful handkerchief, something very simple, or perhaps even a small mark on your body. This will be a constant, positive reminder (always positive), of what you want to emit. For instance, if you're looking for a good job, wearing a brace-*

let that reminds you that you are worthy and deserving of finding it can help. Or if you're at a point in your life where you want to find transcendental spiritual fulfillment, wear a ring that reminds you of that search. The deep feeling of peace will be a great ally.

Remember that psychomagical acts work when they are applied. We are emitting a vibration that reminds us that we need to press the button and generate an even greater vibration.

If you smile at life, life will smile back at you.

TERESA VIEJO

Universal Law III

Principle of Resonance

Within this infinite web we call reality, there are elements that attract each other, generating magnetism and harmony between them.

Once we understand we are part of an immense network, that everything in the universe is connected, and that we are capable generators who can emit and upload information to the great plane of creation, then we are ready to learn about the third principle, which is the Principle of Resonance.

Since you now have discovered the Great Web and also your generative capacity, it is time to recognize that there are parts that pull and attract each other, generating magnetism, a kind of vibrant and fluid dance. This is, in short, the Principle of Resonance.

Now, at this level, resonance is not just about generating but about connecting with what is already generated and attracting to ourselves what is most useful. It is important to know that attracting what you want is possible, beneficial, and achievable if you learn how to do it.

To illustrate this point, consider a river. Creating a new river is vastly different from redirecting the course of an existing one. Is it possible to create a river? Yes, but it would be an immense undertaking, requiring significant modifications to the landscape to generate a new waterway. In contrast, if there is an existing river, we can more easily divert and channel it toward us to reap its benefits. This approach is simpler and, in most cases, far more effective.

One of the principles outlined in *The Kybalion*, one of the most significant esoteric treatises in our history, states that the universe never wastes energy, it moves toward the simplest form that allows it to express itself. What does this mean? For instance, when I decide to walk from my room to my car, I can take ten, twenty, thirty, or fifty steps. I could pass through the kitchen first and then head to the car. I could go through the bathroom, then the kitchen, and then to the car. There are countless paths I could take to reach my vehicle.

The universe, however, operates differently. Unlike humans, who tend to be a bit wasteful of our vital energy, the universe knows how precious energy is and conserves it to the utmost. It never expends energy that is not useful—for this reason, the universe would go directly from the room to the car without deviating, without getting distracted, or without losing energy, always finding the most direct path, the most effective way to reach the result. The universe cares for energy because it is in charge of producing it. We are all responsible for keeping our attention and focus on our goals and going directly toward them.

All living things have a purpose. The universe would never invest its energy in something for nothing. Therefore, you should feel fortunate—if you are here it is because the universe perceives qualities in you that are necessary. We are part of a great orchestra—perhaps just a note or maybe a musical instrument, a small melody or a rhythm, even a moment of silence—but absolutely everyone is an aspect of the great symphony of the universe.

Now, it is important to recognize that, although you are small compared to the immensity of the Great Oneness, you are very important—your vibration and your presence help create and attract the pieces of reality you want in your life.

To illustrate the relationship between the Principle of Generation and the Principle of Resonance, let's consider an example. While the Principle of Generation requires us to expend all our energy to create something entirely new, the Principle of Resonance allows us to invest minimal effort to attract or influence what already exists, aligning it with our goals.

Imagine that each individual on Earth is determined to find a cure for a specific disease. Working in isolation, each person toils away in their own home, without sharing their progress with others. By secluding themselves, they expend an enormous amount of energy, devoting countless hours to making small, incremental progress. This arduous journey would be the inevitable consequence of solely applying the Principle of Generation.

However, by embracing the Principle of Resonance, they could exchange information and leverage the advancements made by others, drawing upon their expertise. This collaborative approach would enable us to integrate our efforts with those of others, connecting with the collective knowledge amassed, ultimately leading to the development of the vaccine or cure. Undeniably, this path would be far more efficient. Wouldn't you agree?

Imagine creating a painting and seeking to complement it with a harmonious array of colors. If the colors you intend to incorporate blend seamlessly, they are said to resonate. If, by some stroke of artistic genius, a particular combination of colors not only blends but also establishes a sense of balance and equilibrium, the resonance is amplified. Perhaps a slightly modified hue perfectly complements the existing palette, achieving an even greater degree of resonance. Therefore, the more closely aligned, the more harmonious the combination, the more balanced and aesthetically pleasing, the greater the resonance.

We can also understand this concept by thinking about music. An E note in one scale differs from an E note in another, yet a commonality binds them—something cohesive, complementary, and perfectly fitting. Similarly, some relationships harmonize effortlessly, bringing comfort and resonance. Others demand far more exertion, lacking the chemistry and connection necessary to create harmony—this is dissonance.

Resonance is an agreement of cooperation. Human beings gain a great deal when we understand this law, when we understand that what we want to attract into our lives can benefit us, but also that what benefits me can benefit others.

We can envision humanity as a universal cooperative where everyone offers something of value. Each individual's contribution enriches the whole, while the collective effort benefits all.

Resonance is inherently multiplicative. Consider the vaccine—imagine the accelerated progress if every scientist and laboratory collaborated openly for the common good. The benefits of shared knowledge are undeniable. It's inspiring to recognize our collective potential when resonance is aligned with a higher purpose.

When you have good intentions for someone and that person has good intentions for you, the sum of those intentions becomes greater. Now, imagine you want to resonate, attract, and connect with abundance, health, and happiness, and with everything that will be good for you. Well, to do this you need to tune in to that energetic frequency from within.

This leads us to the concept of holism. *Holos* is a Greek word that means "whole" or "the sum of all." Holistic means that the whole is greater than the sum of its parts. When a family comes together, they become more than just five individuals. There is something extra that emerges from their union, something that transcends the individual members. In other words, a family is a holistic entity. It is integral, not just a collection of four or five people. It is the energy, the intention, the affection, and the bond that unites them that makes them a family.

Let me tell you a story about resonance. Years ago, a Mexican student of mine told me he had flown to Spain for a renewable energy fair. Thousands of people were milling about the stands, eager to do business. My student was on the lookout for a company that could provide the services he needed, when he spotted a salesman sitting at a desk. The man was one of the hundreds of salespeople at the fair, but something caught my student's attention. As he approached to inquire, he noticed my first published book on the salesman's desk. My student said he hadn't seen the book from afar, but was drawn to it. The story has a happy ending—they made a mutually beneficial deal and both wrote to me about their serendipitous encounter. Two businessmen, one from Mexico and one from Spain, had met at an international fair and discovered they were both my students.

To me, this is an example of resonance—when something about a person's energy can perfectly match the energy of someone else, even if unconsciously.

When we understand that those people we attract are not only attracted by generation, but also by resonance or vibration, we discover why we are so much like our friends. Why we connect with the same type of boss over and over again. Why we attract such similar life experiences, like abuse and abandonment. Or also, why we can maintain a frequency for things and life to go well for us. In the end, we have to be aware that we are in a frequency, attracting similar frequencies—and remember, this is resonance.

HOLOS AND RESONANCE

The concept of holism tells us the whole is greater than the sum of its parts. Now, imagine a band with five members. Each one is an extraordinary musician on their own, but when you hear them play together in harmony, something more is created than the sum of their individual talents. There is an added element, an extra something. The same is true for a car. You can have the tires, the engine, the steering wheel, and the gearshift—but when these elements come together, something greater is created. This is what we call holism.

When you love your partner and they love you back, it's more than just two people loving each other. There's your love and their love, and that creates an even greater love. As Mario Benedetti beautifully puts it, "On the street, side by side, we are much more than two." This added love is exponential and allows us to attract to ourselves everything that matches, resonates, and aligns with that same frequency of love. This is how a loving couple can attract a compatible child, a beautiful home, and a beautiful life.

The universe can vibrate in constructive or destructive resonances. For example, imagine a large space where five people are feeling fear. They begin to emit that feeling, attracting others who resonate with that same fear. As the fear grows, it attracts more and more people who are open to or vibrating at a similar frequency, until eventually the entire space becomes filled with fear through resonance.

Have you ever experienced this at night? Someone says, "I heard a noise," and someone else chimes in, "I felt something too." A collective psychosis begins to build. You start to resonate with the fear. Then someone else hears something new, and the fear escalates, feeding back on itself and resonating more and more because everyone is afraid. If we could divide them, we would realize there is more fear in the room than there are individuals—there is an added fear. This is resonance, attracting different parts to generate more energy.

Let's move on to a positive example. Imagine sitting at your dining table when a family member arrives, exclaiming, "I had a wonderful day! Something amazing happened to me!" And they proceed to tell you all about it. Then, someone else resonates with this good news and shares their own experience: "Well, something similar happened to me, and it was also wonderful." Suddenly, the family starts resonating with positive experiences. Each person shares their own story and the atmosphere becomes filled with a vibrant energy, completely connected to the positive, the pleasant, and the good. This is what resonance is all about. You should seek out positive resonances that will enrich your life and the lives of others.

However, if for some unfortunate reason you find yourself in destructive or negative resonances, such as fear, anxiety, obsession, or panic, remember these three steps that can help you overcome them. I share them with you with all my love.

Overcoming Destructive or Negative Resonance

1. *Remember that everything is part of a whole.*
2. *Consciously generate a constructive vibration that separates you from*

whatever is holding you back. Think a positive thought, make an affirmation, or recall a memory that makes you feel good or grateful for what you have now.

3. *Resonate by vibrating toward what you want to attract. Instead of dwelling in fear, focus on gratitude. Instead of being discouraged, focus on the positive, on the good things that surround you.*

Let's go back to the scenario where a group of people are experiencing fear in a large space. Suddenly, one person in the crowd says, "I firmly believe in light and goodness." This person, by not succumbing to fear, generates a new, constructive vibration with their positive affirmation. They repeat, "I trust in the light and in goodness. Do not despair, because this is good for everyone." With these words, they begin to influence others, resonating with one person after another. Some may still feel fear, while others may feel calm within the same space. But with each person who joins in on the calmness, the vibration starts rising. Remember, you can choose to be swept away by negative resonances, or you can keep your focus high and center on the constructive, vibrating in the positive and attracting people to resonate with the greatest possible good.

THE KEY ELEMENTS OF RESONANCE

The universe is a vast, interconnected web of energy constantly in motion, like a simmering soup. Applying the Principle of Oneness stirs the universe. All of this is part of a vibration. The entire "soup" moves through a code and a frequency. We can understand frequency as the intensity of energy. More energy in less space means a higher frequency. Less energy in the same space means a lower frequency. Vibration and frequency are properties of energy.

Now, back to the soup. In this great soup that is the universe, the constant flow has a rhythm, a kind of background sound, like a drum. That drum is our vibration. Our hearts, which beat in sync with Mother Earth's rhythm, emit a vibration. The spheres in the sky transmit a sound, which is vibration as well. Rotation is also a vibration. A growing plant, though silent, generates a new vibrational pattern. Animals in motion, the sounds of nature, the ocean, a mountain, a stone, the earth itself—all generate vibrations. Everything vibrates.

We can understand this vibration through a measurement called frequency. Frequency is a way of measuring vibration and energy. Frequency allows us to bring a concept from the energetic and spiritual realm onto a tangible plane, and translate it into our own understanding.

We have decided to assign values to completely subjective things, like temperature. In Celsius a healthy body temperature would be 36.5°C. However, in countries that use Fahrenheit, we would have a different measurement that would also indicate good health.

The same is true for weight. If you weigh yourself on a scale that is graduated in kilograms, you will get a different result than if you weigh yourself on a scale that is graduated in pounds. You would have two different numbers for the same weight. So, we assign a value, and from that value we can understand within our own paradigm of perception.

We have assigned values to all things and then legitimized those values as correct. However, the universe is encrypted in much more complex codes of energy and information. If we take a flower or a plant from the garden and want to simplify it into energy, we would have to decode its vibration. We would have to break it down from its original form and give it a subjective energetic value based on its frequency.

Frequencies are essential for understanding how life works from a more transcendent perspective. However, it's important to recognize there are many things that cannot be measured, or that we may not yet have the instruments or tools to do so. There are simply elements that exist, sacred things we cannot encapsulate within our human paradigms.

Illness occurs when a person's frequency of vibration is out of alignment with coherence. In order for you to become ill with a specific condition, you must be vibrating at a frequency that allows this condition to permeate. The easiest example is with viruses and bacteria. In the same room, some people may become infected while others don't. From an energetic perspective, we would say the healthy people are maintaining a high frequency of vibration, which prevents the virus from taking hold.

This same principle can apply to other areas of life as well. For example, if you are vibrating at a harmonious frequency, good things will tend to happen to you. However, if your frequency is low, harmful, or toxic, you may attract complex events through resonance.

In the past, and perhaps even today, knowledgeable people have been able to extract energy from plants. Energy is not the aroma, nor the taste, and sometimes not even the chemical components of plants. It is something more—but it can still be extracted.

Imagine you are a human package of information. This information can be extracted from you in many different ways through vibrations. You can be understood by your height, your weight, and your intellectual qualities. But you can also be understood by your energetic potential and the frequency you are emitting. Perhaps anger or kindness, forgiveness or resentment are also part of a different way of managing the frequencies within you. When you are at peace, substantially calm, your frequency expresses itself in a different way than when you are feeling conflicted or angry, for example.

A mother who yells at her child does not produce the same vibration as when she sings them a lullaby. She is the same person emitting different vibrations, the mother in different expressions.

The universe expresses itself in many ways, but you can choose which frequency to connect with.

In the past, this ability to understand the universe in its range of frequencies was called magic. It was magical when someone gave you a plant or a root, employing its natural energetic qualities to heal you.

Now, when you understand the world through the Principle of Resonance, you can comprehend that it's not just the chemical components of a plant that heal, but its energy and vibration. However, for that vibration to heal you, you must resonate with it. In other words, you must be open to the medicine in order to be healed.

Some say there is no healing without the patient's agreement. This refers to a very simple fact—only when you are internally willing to heal, vibrating in the frequency of healing, can you truly bring healing into your life.

Many people find relief in listening to a Tibetan singing bowl, Gregorian chants, a mass, or even shamanic chanting. However, they don't realize that beneath the melody lies a vibration. It is the energy emitted by this vibration that resonates with you and brings about healing. If singing bowls or chants had inherent healing properties, everyone would be healed by them. But this is not the case. Only those who connect with the deep, the energetic, and the essential receive this medicine. Therefore, you must be aware that when you receive the vibration of the universe, your inner state plays a role in the healing process.

If you are listening to a healing chant and feeling hatred or resentment, or thinking it's nonsense, you will not receive the energy and therefore will not see any effect on yourself. On the other hand, if you are open, receptive, and willing to heal, the energy will heal you through your vibration in coherence with your resonance.

What is commonly known as magic is the art of encoding and decoding the energy of reality. Those who apply Universal Laws to their advantage can achieve seemingly impossible feats. People who can't understand how these feats happen may label them as magic because they seem profound, when they just require the right information and training to perform. However, those of us who do spiritual work—who work with energy, understand the psyche, the mind, and the causes of things—enter planes of consciousness that allow us to resonate with healing, fulfillment, and peace.

ATTRACTING THROUGH RESONANCE

Neurological processes occur through resonance. The synaptic processes that take place inside our brain are electromagnetic processes. When we want to attract something, we can do so from the rational part of our brain by generating energy through our neural flows and constructing phrases like, "I want to have money." Then we think about dollar bills. Using money as a word and dollar bills as an image, we can merge rational energy with mental energy. We can go beyond money and think about what emotion we need to feel to attract abundance. So, we also add emotional energy. Emotions like gratitude, generosity, love, trust, security, fulfillment, joy, happiness, sharing, and peace help.

If I only think of abundance as money, I'm limiting my resonance to just money—bills and coins. If I don't find any bills or coins, I would think there is no abundance. This is a very basic language, where resonance is short: I can only understand abundance as digits and bills. However, if I expand my field of resonance and understand that abundance is bills and coins, yes, but also investments, income, tax breaks, and savings, and if I discover that abundance can come through love, generosity, well-being, even luck, discounts, promotions, and early payments, then I will be able to recognize abundance in more ways and I will be able to resonate with different paths that lead me to it.

If, in addition to these codes and paths, I begin to realize that abundance is beyond what I see, that there is abundance in the love I receive, that abundance is life sustaining us all in its most generous way, that I am abundance, and that being alive, moving, smiling, and enjoying my loved ones is also abundance, I could reach a point where I no longer need money, where I can recognize that the important thing about abundance is not only the tangible codes, what can be touched—if I have found the energetic essence, the vibration behind real abundance—then I start seeing abundance everywhere and realize I am already wealthy.

The money will come as a consequence of the abundance I am vibrating and emitting, as a consequence of the resonance I am generating, because when I resonate with abundance, it wonderfully comes to me.

The same is true for health. If you have a weak immune system, it means you are in greater resonance to attract a number of diseases. On the other hand, if someone has a very strong immune system, it means they have a lower resonance to attract diseases.

When you are sad, your immune system goes down. You resonate with getting sick. When you are happy or joyful, your immune system goes up. Therefore, you resonate less with getting sick. You won't catch the virus or bacteria—you can't attract them—because your vibration and your immune system are rising and preventing you, by vibration, from connecting with the disease.

People who resonate with health tend to be joyful, festive, and grateful. Their immune system constantly receives tokens of affection, and their endorphin production is elevated. Their thymus is at its maximum potential. This person will resonate much more with health and have a low probability of getting sick. To some it may seem like luck, to others mere coincidence, but you, who now understand, will know the answer is resonance. Here are a couple of examples to make things clearer.

EXPANDING YOUR RESONANCE

Imagine a woman who deeply resonates with beauty. She appreciates and takes care of her body, both her external appearance and her emotions. She is beautiful inside and out. This woman goes on a trip with a group of friends. They leave so early, they don't have time to put on makeup or get dressed up. By chance, they have to go straight to a work meeting from the taxi. In the taxi, they see a yellow ribbon. Everyone sees it, but only the woman who resonates with beauty grabs it. When she gets out of the taxi, she simply washes her face and ties her hair back beautifully with the ribbon. She looks stunning.

The question is, why was this woman able to see the same ribbon and use it to vibrate at a higher level of beauty? Through resonance. When you are in contact with beauty, health, abundance, love, and success, you begin to see everything around you as signs, symbols, or amplifiers of this energy. So, if you carry beauty within you, you will reflect beauty outside. And you will find yourself with all the elements that favor or strengthen your beauty.

Another example would be about someone looking for a partner, but they only imagine a potential partner with a specific skin tone, a very precise height, and a particular age. So, they go looking only for that type of person. Can you imagine how many other potential partners they are missing out on? They may end up without a partner at all, because they are unable to open their field of resonance. But if they widen their range of possibilities and understand that a good partner is not limited by age, height, or skin color, but should be a kind, lovely person who nourishes them and whom they can nourish, who respects and loves them, then they can expand their resonance and begin to attract more options. Perhaps even people whom they had not perceived as potential candidates, who were already in their life, may begin to surface because now they can attract them. They are already resonating.

A simple analogy can illustrate this concept. Imagine a shoe salesperson whose focus is limited to selling only shoes. When faced with a crisis or challenging circumstances, their shoe sales decline. At this point, they have two options—maintain their narrow focus on shoes or expand their offerings to include sandals, shoelaces, socks, and sneakers. By broadening their product line, they increase their potential customer base and improve their chances of success. Similarly, by expanding your resonance, you open yourself up to new opportunities and a more positive response from the universe. Therefore, consider whether you are limiting your resonance. Until you realize this potential, your field of possibilities will remain restricted.

I have a specific formula I often use when I desire something. I express my heart's desire exactly as I feel it, but then I conclude with, "And I open myself to the best plan the universe has for me." With this personal expression, I'm essentially telling the universe, "I open my resonance as wide as I can to possibility, but if there's something better for me—something your wisdom intends to send my way that I haven't considered or don't know how to ask for—I'm ready to receive it." If I open myself to possibilities, I allow more energy to find resonance, and there will be greater ease in attracting what I want.

By allowing the universe to guide us, we transcend ego and its limitations, embracing the unifying power of the Principle of Resonance. When we begin to perceive the interconnectedness of the Universal Laws, recognizing our place within a vast network, we espouse the Principle of Oneness. Our ability to influence and create within this network reflects the Principle of Generation. And finally, attracting beneficial resources like a magnet aligns us with the Principle of Resonance.

Now, I would like you to take a few moments to ask yourself: What are you resonating with right now? What are you thinking? What are you feeling?

Your thoughts emit energy into the Great Network, attracting similar experiences. Focus on babies, and you'll encounter them frequently. Dream of a beach vacation, and you'll notice related signs and symbols. Dwell on crisis, and it will magnify. Conversely, thoughts of peace, spirituality, and transcendence open doors to those realms.

These three questions are fundamental: What am I resonating with right now? What am I thinking? What am I feeling?

If life is not bringing you what you want it to bring you, perhaps it is time to apply this principle, and resonate with something new.

Within the realm of transcendental knowledge, there's a concept asserting that everything stems from either love or fear. I can search for a house out of love for a happy family life or out of fear of being without assets. I can approach a partner out of fear of loneliness or out of love for sharing my life with someone special. We might exercise out of fear of gaining weight or out of love for a healthy body. We might go to work out of fear of losing our livelihood or out of love for self-fulfillment and progress.

We must always be aware of what we are generating. If love is at the core of our intention, we will resonate with love in all its forms. However, if fear is present, then we will attract fear in its various manifestations. It's crucial to become self-aware and observe yourself. It's a slow but valuable process to learn to be honest with yourself and ask: Why am I truly doing this? What inner energy is motivating me? Imagine love or fear as the central point from which you vibrate; that vibration will generate a resonance and attract what's deep within your heart—not what your words say or what your actions seem to reflect, but what you're emitting from the depths of your being.

The energy you emit influences an entire system. When you vibrate at a certain frequency, you attract or amplify information and resonate with whatever is in tune with your desire. Your energy field inhabits every thought, every emotion, every idea, behavior, or omission you carry out, and this energy field emanates from you and influences the reality of those around you and the life you experience.

While you are reading my words, perhaps you can perceive the energy emitting from them—the vibrations, the emotions, and the consciousness that are present when I write. Perhaps you can even feel the loving intention and desire to assist you that lies behind them. The more you resonate with my words, the more sense they make to you, the more you accept them within yourself, the stronger the impact they generate in your life.

It is very important to keep in mind that our energy field, which determines our resonance and capacity for creation within the Great Network, is composed of three fundamental elements:

1. The emotions we feel. Remember to keep your emotion centered on love as much as possible.
2. Our mental level. Our thoughts sustain the information we receive and give to and from the world.
3. Our spiritual and transcendent energy.

These three elements, when aligned and coherent, amplify our energy exponentially, enabling us to attract and manifest our desires.

Considering this information, I invite you to ask yourself: What kind of energy field am I creating at this moment? Are my emotions, thoughts, and spiritual energy working in harmony toward a common goal? Am I fully aware of and content with the experiences and circumstances I'm attracting? If not, what adjustments could I make to align my energy with my deepest desires?

Right now, while you are reading, even though we are separated by physical distance, we are connected by the network of oneness, and if you are reading this, it is because something in you and something in me resonates. I hope this book and my words can bring good and light to your life.

Practice to Observe Resonance

At different times throughout the day, I suggest you ask yourself these questions and learn to recognize the answers in yourself:

1. *What is my body emitting? What is my voice emitting? What face am I showing to the world? Are my behaviors kind or aggressive?*
2. *What state of mind am I in now? Am I having positive or negative*

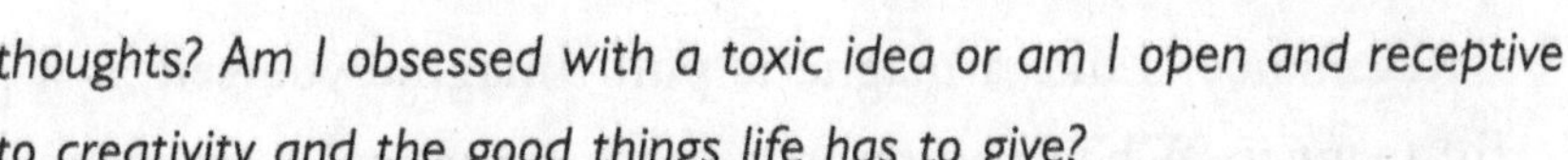

thoughts? Am I obsessed with a toxic idea or am I open and receptive to creativity and the good things life has to give?

3. *What emotions am I experiencing at this moment? Are my emotions open, clear, and filled with light? Am I focused on love? What purpose do these emotions serve in my life now? Are they helping me to fully embrace this present moment?*
4. *On a transcendental and higher level, am I truly at peace with myself, with my surroundings, with life? Do I feel present here and now?*

When you examine yourself and ask these questions, you will gradually become more aware of yourself. Over time, you will gain control over the energy you emit, recognizing that these emissions—pulses and vibrations originating from your emotions and thoughts—directly influence your resonance and ultimately create your reality.

I wish for you a more positive resonance. These laws will teach you, dear reader, that life is generated from what you create within yourself. I suggest performing the above exercise at various times throughout the day. Don't prepare for it—let it arise spontaneously. This way, you'll notice how your resonance shifts in different moments, under various circumstances.

Learning to maintain a harmonious, positive, and constructive resonance is a significant endeavor. It requires great awareness and commitment, but the rewards are extraordinary. When you manage to keep your resonance focused on positivity and light, you'll discover how life begins to mirror the precious light within you.

Be mindful of negative resonance. When you complain, adopt a victim mentality, or have thoughts like "Life is so hard," "This job is exhausting," or "Everything goes wrong," you're resonating with those negative frequencies. As a result, you're more likely to experience fatigue, difficulties, and unpleasant situations.

Resonance is like a magnetic pull. Imagine yourself as a powerful magnet. When you resonate with a particular frequency, you emit a charge that attracts similar energies. If you're emitting a mix of positive and negative frequencies, your experiences will reflect that balance.

When love is placed at your core, your focal point, and your thoughts vibrate in positive and constructive harmony, when your spiritual energy aligns with the greater good and your body reflects this coherence in its actions, then you will be able to attract all the beauty and goodness you desire in your life.

Remember that your actions are producing frequencies—your emotions, thoughts, omissions, everything that is happening—not only frequencies that are seen but also unseen. Therefore, take responsibility, recognize your magnetic influence, and carefully consider your energetic emissions. To a large extent, what you attract is determined by what you emit.

CULTIVATING POSITIVE RESONANCE

I'm going to show you how to cultivate a practice of positive resonance. To optimize your results, consider these four essential elements: thoughts, emotions, intention, and gratitude. Mastering these elements will enable you to attract more of what you desire into your life.

Thought

Imagine you're facing a negative situation and, consequently, your thoughts are negative as well. If, for example, you're unemployed, your first step is to start transitioning your thoughts. Instead of saying, "There's no job," begin opening up to possibility by saying things like, "There are jobs out there for people who are prepared [or lucky, however you want to call it]," or "There are many new opportunities," or "Entire markets are generating options that didn't exist before." Or you could say, "Although it might be difficult to find a job [with that "although," you're introducing a possibility of resonance], enterprising, connected, and open-minded people always find employment."

It's important that you don't jump from a completely negative thought to a positive one, but rather seek an intermediate thought, a possibility. Another example would be thinking, "I'll never get married—I'm already forty." Change that thought to something more like, "Some women or men get married after forty," or "There are people who even get married after fifty, sixty, or seventy." This will open up your mind.

Emotion

The second step is your emotion. You must seek within yourself an emotion that connects you to that job and leads you to believe it is possible. An emotion that is joyful, loving, happy, harmonious. Perhaps one that symbolizes a job that is fulfilling and satisfying. If your emotions reflect anguish, worry, or fear, the resonance will clash between the good intention of your mind and the harmful emotion within you. This is why it is very important to ensure your emotions are as positive and real as you can.

Intention

Third, your intention to find a job should be directed toward something good, useful, and constructive. A job that allows you to enjoy life. A job that allows you to fulfill yourself as a person. A job where you can meet all your needs and desires.

Gratitude

Fourth, finally, it is also important to be grateful for that job, as though it had already manifested. Be grateful for your ability to achieve it—be grateful for life. When we add gratitude to thought, emotion, and intention, we make them much stronger.

Setting Intentions and Expressing Gratitude

Remember this golden rule: always focus your thoughts on what you want to happen. Your emotions should be centered on positivity, and this requires practice. Sometimes, emotions can veer to the negative and thoughts can wander, but it's your responsibility to consciously, attentively, and diligently redirect your thoughts toward your desired outcome and steer your emotions toward what's positive and beneficial for your soul.

To delve deeper, let's understand the concept of intention. Intention is the starting point of your actions, the wellspring of your energy within. Intention gives profound meaning to your actions—it's the deep, authentic, and true purpose that arises from your soul to bring things to fruition.

Often, intention determines the outcome. For instance, when you give money out of pity, the outcome will be vastly different than if you give it out of respect and gratitude. When you say "I love you" from an empty intention, the sentiment is hollow and devoid of meaning. But when you say "I love you" from a full and complete, loving intention, it carries a value that can be perceived. It's a force and an energy that stems not only from the words but from the power of the intention, from the place it arises within you.

To elaborate further on the fourth element, gratitude, understand that it expands energy. When you express gratitude, everything becomes easier. Giving thanks to others for what they give us, appreciating the life we have each day, our bodies, creativity, our mentors and teachers, and moments both simple and grand—all of this elevates our vibrational frequency. The higher this frequency, the greater our ability to manifest, feel a sense of oneness, and resonate with greater precision with what we want to see realized.

To ensure these steps to generating positive resonance are well understood, I want to use this book as an example. It was born from the thought that Universal Laws can benefit everyone. When applied correctly, these laws can enhance our lives and foster growth, transformation, and positive change in both ourselves and those we love.

This book stems from feelings of affection, love, and goodwill. The joy I experience while teaching and sharing my knowledge fills me with a deep sense of fulfillment. This generous spirit is at the heart of this book. The deep purpose of my writing is that you learn a lot, and that what you learn becomes part of your story, part of yourself, and that you apply it to your life. This book's primary purpose is to provide you with a daily tool for understanding and applying these laws, allowing your greatest potential to unfold and manifest positive outcomes. I am grateful to all of you readers who allow my words to resonate with you, my thoughts to inspire you, and our shared humanity to connect us beyond time and space.

Remember, this is a journey. To make these principles a practical part of your life, you must consistently apply and practice them. A helpful reminder is to focus on these four key elements for positive resonance—thought, emotion, intention, and gratitude. This is an ongoing process. Observe yourself closely and ask: What am I vibrating with? How am I vibrating? What am I doing? Align your thoughts with what you desire, ground your emotions in love, set a clear intention, and cultivate gratitude. This will help you manifest a more fulfilling life.

BECOMING AWARE: PRACTICE RESONANCE DAILY

Think about how you might respond when asked, "Do you want abundance? How much abundance do you want? Are you abundant?" Notice how these questions make you feel and what your answers would be.

"Well, as long as life gives me a little," "Just enough to get by," or "Only a little," are responses that create a limited resonance. You're telling abundance, "Yes, but not too much"—but abundance is abundant, not lacking. If you limit abundance, if you block or stop it, you're sending out opposite resonances, actually creating conflict. That's why the correct answer is, "I accept abundance in abundance, fully."

Similarly, what if you were asked, "Do you want to be healthy? How healthy do you wish to be?" If you were to answer, "As long as it doesn't hurt," that answer would be limiting abundance.

Now, expanding on these questions, what happens when you're asked if you're deserving of love, if you want to share a happy life, if you believe in fullness, and if you can feel absolute bliss? If you're capable, worthy, or deserving of living in peace? Observe your answers and become aware. Realize that your responses to life, even if only in your head, are emitting energy and information.

Resonance must be coherent and authentic. You can't fake gratitude—it must be a genuine feeling within you. When you say "I appreciate what life gives me," you must vibrate that gratitude; "I appreciate my family and the people that surround me," you must feel love and think about how good it is to have these people around you; "I appreciate the abundance that comes to me," you have to feel you're not at odds with abundance but rather that you receive it with thoughts, emotions, energy, and intentions all working together so you can say, "Thank you."

If you fake it, only put on a show, or just play a character, the universe will resonate with what you carry within rather than what you display on the outside. If you pretend to like someone but are actually resentful, that person will resonate with your resentment, won't believe you like them, and will be hypocritical, just like you. We must learn to be authentic in our resonance, generating from the depths of our hearts.

What's important now is to understand that if you learn this process, make it a part of yourself, and repeat it over and over, you can begin to consistently express very powerful resonances. If you start to feel gratitude, to think about the positive things gratitude brings to your life, if your intention is to tell the universe, "Thank you," then you will begin to experience many good things coming to you, simply through resonance. Learn to see the world as a space full of possibilities—learn to feel that everything is possible, attainable, and achievable.

Now, we can understand that the Principle of Oneness teaches us we are part of a whole; through the Principle of Generation, we can influence and create something in this whole; and with the Principle of Resonance, we discover that we can attract and vibrate in harmony with what we want to see manifested in our lives.

It is very important that you learn to center your energy, to place yourself in a state of clarity, and to enhance all this energy for the manifestation of what you want to see. We will learn more about this later, in the coming chapters.

We will also discover how to place our energy, to focus so our possibilities of generating and resonating are directed, so we can be like a ship in the vast sea, choosing our route, our destination.

Affirmations for Personal Growth

I'm delighted to share these affirmations with you, to support your personal growth journey.

- *My body expresses the peace within my heart. I trust.*
- *My mind reflects the light of my spirit. I am certain.*
- *My thoughts and emotions work together harmoniously. I am aligned.*
- *My entire being flows effortlessly. I am grateful.*

If what you desire seems uncommon or challenging to manifest, trust that you can create a new reality.

Remember, "impossible" is just a word. Impossible is a word from the world of the rational, the human, and the superfluous. For the universe, nothing is impossible. The possibility of being alive—the possibility of your grandparents meeting; the possibility of your mother, out of so many people, choosing to be with your father; the possibility of the correct sperm reaching the egg; the possibility of you being here reading this book today; the possibility that a meteorite didn't hit the Earth and life is able to continue; the possibility of the perfect distance of the Moon; the possibility that the Earth is at such a precise distance from the Sun that it allows life—is simply impossible.

All of it . . . impossible. And yet, here we are.

Impossible is a construct of the limited mindset we have all put ourselves into. If we were to review the improbable possibility that we, humanity as a whole, have continued living—against all odds—

we would see that we are a direct expression of the impossible. Did you know that, if your mother's temperature had varied a few degrees, you wouldn't be here?

Life is incredible, and I'm happy to think there are many things that are logically impossible—but not for creation!

Even if something is very uncommon, it may yet be possible and attainable. If you maintain an open mindset, opportunities will come your way and miracles will unfold. You are learning Universal Laws, you are stepping outside the box, you are entering the world of uniqueness, learning about creation and resonance.

Remember, a philosophy that should guide you in life is: "Be open to possibility." Don't close the universe off to opportunities. You may not fully understand how it works, but for now, don't limit all the good that can come. Always trust the universe has paths that, though they may seem impossible to the mind, can and will occur for your highest good.

If what you desire is scarce, don't be discouraged because, little by little, as you seek it, you will generate the possibility and resonate with the wonderful energies that will accompany you in finding your goal. With scarce things, we need to be more patient, firm and attentive with our intentions. If there's a possibility it can happen, why couldn't it happen to you? The following story exemplifies this.

I had a high school teacher to whom I feel I owe a great deal. He taught Spanish at a school in Mexico City and was the only one among my teachers who accepted and understood what others considered my "quirks."

I hadn't told anyone that I had the gift of clairvoyance. I was already going through puberty, a complete mess, and couldn't control this gift of vision. One day, this teacher said to me, "I get the feeling you feel very alone. Is that right?" From then on I began to open up to him, and that's how this man, who started out as my Spanish teacher, became my confidant and spiritual mentor.

I told him I had the ability to see things, and he helped me understand a lot more about this gift and myself. He was one of the few adults who truly listened to and understood me. I want to share his story with you, to honor how much this great man did for me. The things I will say about him are said with the utmost respect.

My teacher was born in Oaxaca, in a rather poor Indigenous community. His father had also been a rural teacher in Mexico, ninety years prior. As a child, my teacher suffered from polio, which caused severe atrophy in his lower limbs. His legs were short, and doctors predicted a life of immobility, illness, and social exclusion.

But my teacher's father was an unrelenting man. Due to the deformities caused by polio, my teacher had severe motor difficulties, but when he was a child and asked his father to help him move around, the man would harshly tell him to just crawl.

"Please, Dad, help me get into bed."

"Crawl!"

"Dad, I want to go outside."

"Crawl!"

The man was tough, and childhood was a very painful stage both physically and emotionally for my teacher. He attended a rural school and had to crawl everywhere by himself. Without proper medical devices, moving this way was not only difficult and embarrassing but also led to excessive development of his back and hands, which further contributed to his striking appearance.

When he reached adulthood, there weren't many opportunities to thrive in his village—the most one could aspire to was becoming a school teacher. To achieve this, he had to study to be a rural teacher. My teacher dedicated himself to this, just as his father had done.

After finishing school with great sacrifice, and obtaining his degree as a rural teacher, he came crawling to his father and showed him the diploma. "Look—despite your mistreatment, I managed to become a rural teacher," he said.

Then his father replied, "Not despite me, but because of me. Crawl!"

"Why are you still so harsh?" my teacher asked him.

"If I had carried you everywhere in my arms for even a day, you wouldn't have gotten here. It's because I made you crawl that you got here," his father replied.

My teacher, by crawling, arrived in Mexico City and obtained a teaching position.

"Why don't you walk?" he was asked once.

"Well, because I have polio," he replied, looking at his small legs. "And because I've been crawling all my life."

"And have you never tried to walk?" they insisted.

"No, I only know how to crawl," said my teacher.

"What if you learned to walk?" they questioned.

This question kept echoing in his head, to the point that, at thirty years old, he managed to start walking with the support of a cane. My teacher could finally move with his own legs. Some decades later, when I met him, he walked a little crooked but no longer used a cane.

He nicknamed me "*Camellito*," which in Spanish means "little camel." One day he came up to me and said, "Camellito, even if they tell you that you can't walk, stand up and try!"

Today, I repeat these words to you: "Stand up and try." I don't know if it will take you thirty years, but I'm sure that, with dedication and love, you'll be able to do whatever it is you set your heart to.

When you plant a seed of love,
it is you that blossoms.

MA JAYA SATI BHAGAVATI

Universal Law IV

Principle of Karma

Every action has a reaction. Everything we do has consequences; recognizing and taking responsibility for these consequences allows us to grow.

Karma is a principle that originates from the Hindu tradition. Its name comes from Sanskrit and means "action." The Principle of Karma is also known as the Principle of Causality, and although many people talk about karma, few truly understand it.

We have misused this word, assuming that karma means that if you hit someone, someone will hit you back; that if you steal from someone, someone will steal from you. This is overly simplistic and absurd. Karma is a more complex principle, as we will discover in this chapter.

All the things that happen to us—the cheerful experiences, the painful ones, the important people we meet to grow or to learn from, the most glorious moments, and the events that touch our soul—have a purpose, are part of a grand project, and it is up to us whether we cooperate, flow, learn, and transcend challenges, or if we simply let ourselves be dragged along by circumstances.

We must become aware that we are here for a reason and that the things we are experiencing, whether difficult or easy, complex or simple, have a purpose—to teach us something we need to learn.

We need to let go of the basic, simple, and incomplete idea that karma is solely about the bad things that happen to you or an identical response to the things you've done (you were deceived because you deceived, you're suffering because you made someone else suffer), and open ourselves to understanding that karma is much vaster, much more complex, and profoundly more significant for our lives.

Every action is karma. Eating breakfast creates karma, not eating breakfast also creates karma, desiring breakfast creates karma, and thinking about breakfast creates karma. Every action carries energy; therefore, everything we experience, everything we do, will generate an effect, and that effect is karma.

So, if you do something, you produce karma, but if you don't do it, you also produce karma. If you have the intention or desire but don't carry it out, you are emitting karma. If you do a good deed, if you help, if you have a loving intention, you are also generating karma. If you want to help, that intention generates karma, but if in addition to wanting to help, you actually help, care, and protect, then the karma is amplified.

Let me give you an example. Imagine you find a tiny abandoned plant on the street—your desire to help generates karma. But you don't just stop at the simple desire, you go get the plant, rescue it, and then you generate the karma of the desire plus the karma of the rescue. Then you take it home and pot it up it with great care—

generating more positive karma. You water it, put it in the sun, and make sure it grows. Just as the plant will grow and expand, so too will karma, due to the sum of good deeds. From intention to action, support, care, idea, and desire, everything we emit is pulsating with energy, and karma is the effect of all those energies you are generating.

Therefore, absolutely everything we experience produces an energetic effect, and this energetic effect is karma. The amount of energy we produce will generate an amount of karma—so, if you have desire, intention, action, purpose, and meaning, you are making your karma broader.

It is essential to recognize that desires, intentions, and purposes can create as much or more karma as the action itself. For example, a doctor who operates with the intent to save a patient but inadvertently causes their death incurs karma for both the benevolent intention and the harmful outcome. Both actions generate karmic consequences.

I invite you now to reflect on your daily activities and your life's work. Consider the energy your actions generate. When your pursuits nurture and protect life, you generate karma. If you do nothing to improve the condition of the people who work with you, you generate karma. If you defend and create a union to support them, you generate karma. If in that union you profit from the workers' money and misuse it, you also generate karma. There is the karma of good intention and the karma of abuse. With this, I want to make clear that everything we emit (actions, emotions, thoughts, and desires) is generating energy, and that energy will have an effect that we call karma.

Something I would like to share with you is that I didn't learn the Universal Laws solely from books or self-inquiry. It was while being in India that I discovered karma. Being there in its cradle, from the place where the philosophy of karma was generated, allowed me to take a precious approach. I discovered, for example, that people in that country accept that there are different levels of evolution and different types of karma.

A swami, an Indian master, once told me, "If a person is consistently seeking the truth and doesn't find it, they have merit for their search, for their desire to find it. If a person isn't seeking the truth and finds it, they have the merit of having found it. But when a person is seeking the truth and finds it, they have the merit of the search and the merit of the finding. Of the three, who has the most and best karma? The answer is the third one, because they sought and found. And between the one who found it and the one who sought it? The one who sought it with a deep desire has better karma than the one who only found it by chance."

When I remember that experience, I think of a very sacred mountain, Arunachala. My journey to this place was a turning point in my life because I learned to understand the deep meaning of *dharma* and karma. On this journey of the infinite soul, there, in the deepest parts of rural India, I met an enlightened presence who showed me the path to awakening.

Today, as I write this book, I know, according to the Hindu tradition, that this great saint has even more karma in his favor now because he inspired me. The teaching he left in me is reaching you through this book. Every person who becomes aware of karma and improves their life because of this book is adding merit to that precious person I discovered under a tree, in the absolutely fascinating and enchanting India.

In the Western world we live in, surrounded by so much concrete and so little philosophy, we view life in a very flat, very immediate sense. We are accustomed to being offended because we had a bad experience, to becoming frustrated because something didn't go the way we wanted, to filling ourselves with rage because a difficult circumstance crossed our path, to feeling deeply hurt when our plans didn't materialize as we had dreamed. We think there is injustice behind these acts, that the universe simply woke up on the wrong side of the bed and wanted to harm us. However, when we understand the law of karma, we become aware that what is happening may be the effect of something we had sown previously. Perhaps this action you see as bad is nothing but a gift, something very good that is coming to you later. Or, probably, this adverse circumstance is the effect of the seeds you planted.

Please understand that the many blessings that surround you are partly karma, that the beautiful family you have now is the karma of having taken care of them, of having been present, of having given your best. That perhaps the professional success you enjoy is the effect of having sown many evenings of study, dedication, passion, and complete commitment to your work.

Karma eradicates the idea of luck because it makes us responsible for understanding that the good and bad we are experiencing are perhaps effects of causes we sowed, of intentions and purposes, of actions and awareness we experienced in the past.

Imagine you believe your lack of a partner stems from the universe's cruelty, a sense of cosmic injustice. Now take a deep breath and examine yourself. Perhaps you have a lot of fear, and that fear of finding love sows or generates, as a consequence, the lack of a partner in your life. Maybe a childhood wound hinders your ability to connect joyfully with a partner. Perhaps, consciously or unconsciously, you've rejected many people who have approached you, and what you now see as an injustice for which you're not responsible—feeling that there's no partner because of bad luck or a curse—is nothing more than the effect of the causes you've sown.

However, it also gives us hope. If karma reveals that life responds to the intentions, purposes, desires, and actions we generate, this means if we sow seeds of peace, light, and love, we will reap precious fruits that correspond directly to these seeds.

On the other hand, imagine a very successful person in her profession, recognized and valued, a female executive who is very important to her organization. From the outside, you might say, "She's lucky," or "Sure, stuff like that just happens to her." Perhaps it was simply coincidence, but deep down all those who know a successful person know that success was sown many years ago, perhaps when they were in high school, perhaps when they chose a complex career in university and learned to speak two or three languages. Or in the many mornings they got up early to give their best, or the late nights they spent toiling, or the extracurricular activities where they forged and formed themselves, and the relationships they weaved over time. And so, instead of seeing success as a product of life's circumstances, we understand it as the fruit of constant work.

Likewise, instead of seeing painful circumstances as mere luck, we assume perhaps there is a part of us that influenced the causes that resulted in these effects.

Now, think of yourself as part of a network—that is the Principle of Oneness; we generate intentions, thoughts, and desires with our energy—the Principle of Generation; we can attract or connect with things that can bring us greater good in life—the Principle of Resonance; and we are responsible for the effects of what we have generated and can generate new seeds to sow wonderful effects—this is karma.

Why can't we understand the laws of karma? What are we missing to be able to discover this wonderful principle in the everyday life we live?

The answer is simple—we lack time and consciousness. Contemporary humans, trapped in the frenetic pace of city life, possess narrow minds and shortsighted perspectives. Let me explain. We perceive events in a purely immediate manner. For example, "I twisted my ankle—how unlucky!" But perhaps we fail to notice that, before this painful injury, we had taken missteps two or three times in the same week. Life was sending us warnings to be cautious. Twisting an ankle is not solely the street's fault but also a consequence of inattention, distraction, and the habit of walking while glued to our cell phones.

A sprained ankle is the universe's response to your lack of bodily awareness, to your inability to step with certainty. It's not about self-reliance but rather about influencing outcomes through different energy levels. Faced with difficulties, we often dramatize and become indignant, feeling unfairly victimized. But perhaps the issue isn't injustice.

Let's consider our experience of the COVID-19 pandemic. We felt isolated in our suffering, forgetting that every generation faces its own trials. Perhaps this pandemic was a karmic consequence of our collective selfishness and fragmented worldview, a stark reminder of our shared vulnerability. Death knows no wealth, race, or status.

This crisis demanded a shift from selfishness to collective responsibility. Personal desires must sometimes yield to the greater good. The story is simple—if you believe that events are not random, you are awakening to the concept of karma—every effect has a cause. A sculpted physique is the product of dedicated training, while obesity and diabetes often result from poor habits, physical problems, or a lack of self-love. Business success is built on diligence, intellect, strategy, and talent. Let us embrace the core of karma—responsibility.

THE THREE GENERATORS OF KARMA

There are three generators of karma—intention, action, and situation. Let's see how they work.

Let's say I dislike someone and decide to harm them. I make a salad with rotten avocado and give it to them to eat. That spoiled avocado gives them indigestion and they have to go to the hospital. At the clinic, they detect a serious condition they would never have noticed if they hadn't gone for a checkup. Thanks to the visit to the hospital, they detect liver cancer that can be treated because it is in the early stages. So, going to the hospital saved that person's life. My initial intention to harm them turned into their salvation. How many karmas will I pay, one or two? Actually, both actions carry karmic weight—the malevolent intent, and the accidental kindness.

Karma is like a ledger—every action performed can be a debit or a credit. In the Hindu tradition, actions that are good and bright are called dharmic acts. In reality, the same action can have mixed karmic consequences. We are discussing not only the Principle of Karma but also the Principle of Generation. And as everything influences and is connected to everything else, understanding that all things are expanding in oneness results in the Principle of Resonance and Oneness as well. We have grasped the first four principles.

Now, I want you to think about your own life experiences, when someone trying to harm you has actually done you good, or someone trying to do you good has caused you conflict. Perhaps someone you once loved left you, abandoned you, hurt you, and broke your heart. But by leaving you, they allowed you to meet someone else who made your life immensely happy, with whom you found love and started a family. So, was that harm of being left really harm, or did it bring good consequences to your life?

Maybe you've heard of people who are given a promotion, which seems promising and wonderful—there's more money, abundance, and recognition. But that promotion ends up destroying their inner self, leading to disorder, depression, alcoholism, and inner ruin. Therefore, it's very important to understand that karma is always present and that the seeds we sow bear multiple fruits—that in life there's usually nothing that is "only good" or "only bad."

To understand karma, you must meet one condition: take responsibility.

Karma is action. In everything we generate, think, and do, there is karma. The energy that derives from our actions, thoughts, emotions, consciousness, omissions, labors, and services is karma. Everything you do generates energy; every time energy is generated, it produces a stimulus, and that stimulus gives a response—this is karma.

So, is karma an energy of cause or of effect? The answer is resounding—it's both. Karma is cause *and* effect. Karma is a cause when it produces an effect, and becomes an effect when it comes from a cause. Everything we experience is an endless cycle of causes and effects.

I initiate a conflict, thereby incurring karmic responsibility. When others become involved, they too are ensnared in this karmic web. Escalating the dispute through aggression amplifies my karmic debt. However, if they respond with violence, they also generate karmic energy. This back-and-forth exchange creates a cycle of giving and receiving, of actions and consequences. We become both instigators and victims within this endless flow of karma.

Now, imagine me saying to you, "I reprimanded my friend because something they did hurt me." What is the cause—their action that caused me pain, or my subsequent retaliation? My retaliation was a result of their hurtful behavior. But they might argue that they hurt me because I didn't answer the phone earlier. So, the cause—not answering their call—led to their anger, which resulted in their hurtful action toward me. My subsequent retaliation then triggered another hurtful response from them.

This becomes much simpler when we understand cause and effect. We must recognize that everything in life has an effect and a cause, that everything is interconnected. A single karmic action can be amplified, expanded, or multiplied. We also hold the power to create new, calming influences. When I apologize, I alter the flow of bad karma; when I take responsibility or choose peace over conflict, I emit a new, more bright karma. If the other person connects with this intention—to stop arguing, to acknowledge, to assume responsibility, and to prioritize love—we shift from the destructive karma of violence to a virtuous karma of order, peace, and goodness.

Do you realize how powerful our thoughts are? How strong the Principle of Generation is? Can you recall a situation in which, caught in a destructive and violent cycle of karma, you chose peace? By choosing peace, did you generate new causes that led to new effects, thus transforming a painful karma into a virtuous one in which everyone involved could grow?

Karma is cause and effect—sometimes cause, sometimes effect. Every cause produces an effect, and every effect comes from a cause. Let me tell you something—those of us who are passionate about history find it very difficult to explain it, because history is a chain of causes and effects. Imagine World War I. What was the cause? The assassination of Archduke Franz Ferdinand of Austria. But in reality that death was the effect of an oppressed society seeking a way to express its pain in the face of an authoritarian empire. We could also say that oppressed society was the effect of many centuries of conflict in that part of the world, and so on—we could go back, recognizing that every cause was, in turn, an effect.

The same thing happens with our personal story. If you're angry, anger is both an effect and a cause. It can be the effect of traffic and the cause of a family argument. Do you realize this?

There's no way to avoid generating energy. If a person shuts down and remains silent in the face of an unpleasant circumstance, their silence and seclusion are emitting energy. Have you heard of "passive aggression"? Of people who don't insult or shout, but who hurt with their behavior? Do you think there's more karma in a shout than in a harmful action? The answer is simple—we are constantly generating karma, whether we're doing something or doing nothing. But please, don't worry, don't obsess. On the contrary, understanding karma means understanding we are responsible for the effects in our lives, that we can play with them positively and keep sowing the beautiful seeds of the splendid life we want to live.

Everything we do generates karma. I often think about a very difficult period in my life in which, through no fault of my own, I lost everything. When I think back to that time, with my level of consciousness back then, I experienced it as a great injustice, with deep pain. Due to conflicts between my parents, which were beyond my control, I was left without a home or school—I was left on the street. However, as time passed, I reasoned that, thanks to that difficult circumstance, I had to mature very early and become a very responsible and hard-working man. Before I turned twenty-one, I was already supporting myself; I became a man at a very young age.

From the level of consciousness I have today, I realize that, actually, that adverse personal circumstance brought much good to my life. If my parents had acted differently, they would have emitted a different karma for me and this would have brought a different life than the one I have today. Now I can be grateful that things happened as they did, because I learned a lot from the difficult experiences.

I believe when we look at things that happened to us—including complicated or negative ones—over time and with awareness, we discover they brought good seeds. Therefore, let's stop being afraid of karma. Everything we do or don't do will generate karma, so our attention should be focused on learning to generate good karma—this is where consciousness and inner work come in. This is where the law of karma works to your benefit by cooperating to create the best version of yourself and the fullest life you can aspire to.

GENERATING GOOD KARMA

In Hindu philosophy, when someone performs a compassionate act from the depth of their heart, and helps another purely out of companionship and selflessness, this generates a wonderful energy—virtuous, positive, bright karma. When someone has extended a helping hand in a difficult moment, that person's act has undoubtedly been noted by the universe and will return to them positively.

We must remember that the energy we emit encompasses not only our actions but also our thoughts and feelings—the intention and energy generated from within each of us.

Karma can be classified in many ways. One classification identifies four types: physical, mental, emotional, and transcendental.

Physical karma is easy to see. How we treat our bodies directly impacts their condition. Discipline, a balanced diet, sufficient sleep, daily exercise, mindful breathing, and consistent care can contribute to a healthy old age. This is not coincidence but rather the result of years of bodily kindness. Conversely, poor sleeping habits, late nights, disorganization, unhealthy eating, sedentarism, and excessive alcohol consumption can lead to physical decline. Difficulty moving or organ failure are not coincidences but rather consequences of mistreating the body.

Some mental karmas are quite subtle, influenced by the direction of one's thoughts. It can be helpful to ask, "Why are these bad things happening to me?" Then, delve deeper to recall where your thoughts were at the precise moment these things happened.

I recommend to my students that whenever they have an accident—a fall, a cut, a burn, or a bruise—they immediately ask themselves, "What was I thinking about? Where was my attention?"

Many times, you will discover the things that are happening to you are linked to the thoughts you are generating, and the effects you see manifested in life are the answer to your mental level.

Emotional karmas are directly tied to our present feelings. Choosing a pet motivated by loneliness yields different results than choosing one out of a desire to provide a home and companionship. It also differs from selecting a pet based solely on appearance, viewing it as an accessory. As discussed in the Principle of Resonance, each emotion, starting point, and intention produces distinct karmas.

Examining the emotions that drove past or current relationships can be illuminating. Honesty is key here. Was it fear, low self-esteem, arrogance, deep love, or a longing for balance and harmony? This introspection reveals how emotions shape outcomes.

Let's delve a little deeper. If I feel fear, it transforms into energy that generates more fear. Through resonance I attract fear, and through karma I experience its effects. Imagine these Universal Laws working together: I feel fear, I generate fear, I resonate with fear, and I encounter fearful responses.

This phenomenon is quite common in life. A child who fears being bullied, who feels weak, emits a vibration that attracts abuse and bullies. Consequently, they often end up being hurt. It's terrible.

Now let's do the exercise in a positive and inverse way. If you have feelings of peace in your heart, if you truly feel peace from deep within, you will generate a peaceful energy around you, but you will also attract events, books, podcasts, and friends who are at peace like you, resonating with them, and the effects in your life will also be peaceful and calming. It's important to realize that, by understanding Universal Laws, you can begin to influence your reality so the things you desire most can happen.

Universal Laws can also conflict when feelings of lack coexist with intentions of abundance. Simultaneously resonating with the fear of loss and the desire to gain creates a chaotic internal landscape. Conflicting life directives—spend, save, invest, enjoy responsibly—further exacerbate this disorientation. The root of this confusion lies in the misconception that these principles must function independently rather than harmoniously.

When you feel confident in yourself, emit certainty in your ability, resonate with self-worth, and have as your purpose the finding of abundance in an honorable and dignified way, all your systems work in the same direction. Your generation, your resonance, and your karma align with the Principle of Oneness to bring you the most beautiful circumstances, abundance, appreciation, recognition, trust, and certainty. That's what learning the Universal Laws is about, putting them into practice for the service of our greatest good.

Karma occurs on two fundamental levels—the material and the

spiritual. The karma of the material plane is evident in an immediate and daily way. It is what manifests when you overeat and then get indigestion, or when you overspend and accumulate a lot of debt. Or if, for example, you built a house on the edge of a cliff or near a riverbed, and when it rained, the house collapsed or flooded. And you might complain about life's injustice, when from the beginning you knew that if you built there, something like that could happen.

When a population is incoherent and indolent, a similar type of president often emerges through a process of resonance. Conversely, a cultured and educated populace tends to elect a similar kind of ruler. The resulting karma is that the people suffer the consequences of their chosen leader, failing to recognize that they themselves incubated the conditions for such a government.

Material karma is practical, visible, and relatively swift. It can be instantaneous and tangible, the karma of life's simplest things. Forgo a sweater on a cold day, and you might catch a chill. Call it karma or carelessness, as you prefer. Neglect to cultivate an organized work system, and you'll likely face a heavy workload and increased pressure at month's end. Is it fate, or the result of failing to sow the right seeds of order and discipline? Similarly, sudden weight gain or insurmountable debt often stems from a gradual accumulation of small, unconscious decisions.

On the other hand, spiritual or energetic karma exists on a completely different, much higher level. It is a timeless karma that does not immediately manifest. Unlike its material counterpart, this karma lacks a direct meaning or concrete cause. We may perceive it as something inexplicable. For instance, how can a person who has worked diligently and responsibly their entire life not experience abundance? Such a person might wonder, "Why is this happening to me? Why haven't I achieved the desired results despite doing everything right?"

Perhaps this is a matter of spiritual karma, as difficult experiences can sometimes precede positive outcomes. Initially, this concept may be challenging to grasp, but careful observation reveals how threads of adversity can weave into a tapestry of harmony and peace.

For example, the death of someone I loved deeply is a tangible, physical manifestation of karma. I'm consumed by anger because that person was so important to me, and their loss is both painful and enraging. I can only perceive the pain now, but I believe there's a profound, underlying reason for their departure—a reason I may not grasp in my current state of anger. Perhaps time, or even my own death and subsequent enlightenment, will offer clarity.

Spiritual karma doesn't have a quick or immediate reaction, and sometimes its causes are beyond our consciousness. Let me give you an example.

I once had a patient who couldn't get pregnant. She was frustrated. She was undoubtedly a very good person with a good husband, living a good life, and trying desperately to conceive, but she couldn't achieve her goal.

Medically, there was no physical reason why the pregnancy couldn't happen. She was very religious and prayed a lot to God. She didn't understand why two good people who loved each other so much and would be responsible parents couldn't have a child. And the woman looked back and couldn't remember any action she might have taken that would prevent her from getting pregnant.

Over the course of several sessions, we learned that the woman had undergone multiple abortions as a teenager. She had expressed a clear desire not to become a mother, and the universe respected that choice. We did not judge her. Yet, unbeknownst to her, these experiences had planted subtle seeds of resistance to motherhood. Subsequently, working with her husband, we uncovered a deep-seated economic anxiety in him. He was fearful of financial instability and its impact on fatherhood, but had suppressed these concerns. Together, the woman's history and the man's hidden fear created subtle barriers to conception. Remember the concepts of generation and resonance? These dynamics were at play in their lives.

After a period of focused effort during which the woman conducted rituals to heal and bring peace to her aborted children and the man overcame his fear, they unexpectedly conceived without medical intervention. They now have three children. This outcome suggests they resolved their underlying issues by gaining awareness of and healing past karma.

It is also necessary to mention collective karmas. Countries, religious groups, and ethnic groups possess them. Japan, a nation I deeply admire, serves as a prime example. After the devastating moral and economic losses of World War II, this country rose from the ashes to create a society renowned for its order, discipline, and ethical values. Japan resolved to end the conflict's destructive effects, including hunger and the total devastation wrought by seeds of superiority, domination, ego, and control. Instead, it sowed new seeds of peace, coupled with technology, hard work, and discipline. In just fifty years, this former wartime loser, akin to Germany, transformed into a world power. How did Japan achieve this? Not through luck or geography, but through the labor and cultivation of its people.

Many countries are immensely wealthy in resources yet impoverished in philosophy and moral values, with dysfunctional economies and authoritarian or weak governments. Is this merely fortune? I think not. It is karma, and it is incumbent on all of us to consciously cultivate the energy we wish to sow in order to reap the desired karmic rewards.

When we talk about karma, we have to eradicate the dualistic idea of positive and negative, of thinking things are simply good or simply bad, and understand that everything is intertwined. The universe doesn't think in terms of good and bad—it thinks in terms of energy.

By giving you this information and making you responsible for your karma, you may become obsessed, feel trapped and limited, taking what you read as something negative. But you can also use this book from a responsible, constructive, and creative position, and then, from the depths of your being, begin to sow the best seeds. Therefore, by sharing all this, I trust that in the vast majority of cases I will generate positive karma because I am sharing information that will help you improve your lives and the lives of those around you. In this way, by planting small seeds, we cultivate love.

Imagine a father's disappointment upon learning the strict education he'd believed essential for his children was in fact a source of pain for them. Undoubtedly, he sowed seeds of order and discipline with the best intentions, but his children experienced these as harsh. How many karmic forces are at play here? Certainly, the parent's noble purpose of raising and educating his children generates positive karma. However, the children's pain is also significant and must be considered, resulting in a less bright karma.

When we look back at our history, we must become aware of the seeds we have sown and maturely accept the results they have brought to our lives.

I'm going to share three fundamental premises with you. If the life you have is good, recognize and applaud the seeds you've sown. If it's sometimes good and sometimes bad, correct what's been sown poorly and plant good things. And if you don't like the life you have or it's not taking you where you want to go, then start sowing new paths so the road straightens out and you can, in time, live as you want.

It's not enough to simply say we're never going to emit bad karma—that's impossible—but we can avoid, as much as our consciousness allows, harming, destroying, deceiving, or hurting others. It's sometimes difficult to know if the actions we take may have a harmful impact on others but, as far as our conscience and personal power allow, we can do everything with the intention of generating the greatest good for others. When karma is very good, we are following our dharma (more on dharma in the next chapter).

I wish we were all mindful of the seeds we're sowing. Some bear negative fruit, while others yield positive results. Ultimately, the key is to plant so many positive seeds, even if a few negative ones take root the overall outcome will be harmonious and dharmic for you.

Perhaps it's easier for us to admit we've hurt others—educated our children poorly or been bad spouses, bad parents, bad women, bad men—because this is socially correct. Perhaps it's much harder for us to acknowledge all the good we've done in our lives.

I propose you review the many good deeds you have done for others, such as providing employment, being honorable, telling the truth, being very kind to someone who needed you, working hard, caring for people close to you, being close to your grandparents, treating a child with love, protecting the defenseless. Please don't see yourself from a totally dark perspective. I'm sure you've used most of your energy from a good place, and it's been for something good and useful.

ARE WE DOOMED?

Given what you've read, you may wonder whether you're destined for a life of bad karma, like the destructive kind you may be experiencing now, or if you'll forever bear the consequences of past mistakes. I can categorically say, "No." You have the power to redeem and restructure your karma. As long as there's life, we can consciously or unconsciously purify our karma, even renegotiate it. Imagine going to a "karma bank" and saying, "Look, I owe this much, but I have these assets to my credit. Can we work out a manageable payment plan?"

The world's karma may respond, "Be careful not to go into debt again. Be responsible and stop gossiping or being nosy. Dedicate yourself, perhaps once a week, to praying for the planet or helping someone in need."

You can create a program to pay off negative karma, by investing in positive karma. I insist, we shouldn't fall into the temptation of labeling karma as "bad" or "good." On the contrary, we should assume it has many threads, and start from the vital truism that what we do comes from love. As I taught you in the Principle of Generation, attracting whatever is best in our lives, such as with pure resonance and by connecting with the Great Network of oneness, will create a place that generates the best possible karma.

However, we tend to complain about our personal histories. We lament a partner's departure, overlooking how it led to a more fulfilling love. We pity that a man's war wounds forced him to retire. Yet, we might consider that those injuries allowed him to immerse himself in transformative journey—as Saint Ignatius of Loyola's led him on the path of becoming a saint.

This is why I ask you to stop judging life in terms of good or bad. Do not view illness as inherently positive or negative. Stop analyzing leaders solely through the lens of good or bad. Instead, seek the positive within the negative. Always, in complex situations, there are glimmers of light to be found that foster knowledge, awareness, and growth.

You can even—and this requires a compassionate perspective—

look back at the difficult, harrowing circumstances you've endured. Sometimes it's challenging to find the good in experiences that have caused us pain. But you might ask yourself, "What did I learn from this? What was the universe trying to teach me?" Then, with careful attention, observe the positive outcomes that emerged from the negative. Believe me when I say that, once we begin this process, we realize life is not a dualistic struggle but a complex, wondrous system. According to the Principle of Oneness, everything the universe offers is meant to contribute something and teach us something.

The seeds of the past have an impact on your present, and the ones you sow in your present will shape your future. Instead of lamenting what you've already done, focus on creating a new path toward a full life, with love and with your best intention.

THREE TYPES OF KARMA

Karma is not a singular, simple concept. Instead, the concept of karma encompasses various types, each with distinct effects, purposes, and timelines. We will now examine three of these types: ancestral karma, present karma, and destiny karma.

Ancestral karma comes from our families, our ancestors, or perhaps from our past lives for those who believe in reincarnation. You might think of it as the legacy we've inherited from generation to generation.

Present karma is the most important. It refers to what I am generating here and now, what I am producing with my actions, my intentions, my thoughts, my behaviors—both the noblest and, of course, the darkest parts of me. This is the karma we should focus on the most.

Destiny karma is a divine, predetermined karma beyond our

control. It constitutes only 2 percent of our total karma but is nonetheless crucial. This type of karma is linked to our birthplace and parents. A disability or unique abilities might be attributed to destiny karma.

We must always remember that we cannot control karma, we can only direct our actions in the most positive way we know how. For instance, I cannot predict the impact of this chapter. I do not know if it will be well-received, cause discomfort, be utilized, harm anyone, or inspire new possibilities. What I can control is my intention and purpose in sharing it in this book and my courses. Good intentions do not guarantee positive outcomes. I do not act with malice, but I cannot predict the karmic consequences. I can only be certain of my actions—the seeds I sow.

I'll tell you a little more about these three types of karma.

Ancestral Karma

Ancestral karma refers to the role your family has given to the social, cultural, economic, and religious situation in which you were raised—your belief system, your phobias and likes, your attachments, and your desires are partly influenced by the education you received. If you grew up in a dignified home, with well-educated, prepared, and well-intentioned parents, your destiny will be different than if you were born into a dysfunctional home, with sick, toxic, uneducated parents with limited consciousness. If you had been raised in another religious, social, or cultural environment, or if instead of a good education you received mistreatment from your parents or felt abuse instead of cooperation, that would undoubtedly have influenced the life you live now.

We often view ancestral karma solely through a negative lens, focusing on perceived inherited burdens, guilt, or judgments, or perhaps, even suffering the judgments of others for belonging to our family. Yet, we also inherit values, educational opportunities, love, support, affection, table manners, and the fundamental gifts of food and shelter—all of which are also forms of ancestral karma.

The surname passed down to us, along with its reputation—good or bad—our own name, and the place our parents and grandparents granted us in society, all of that is part of ancestral karma. We must learn to be grateful for it, because none of us made by ourselves. Much of what we have obtained over the years was partly given to us by the foundations our families provided. It is important you learn to honor and appreciate the history from which you came.

Karma is more like a river than a drop of water—it keeps flowing. You cannot separate a cause from an effect, which in turn generates another cause and produces a new effect. It is important to know that things that seem terrible can end up being marvelous.

Generally, the karma that has been given to us has been useful and good. And as we grow, we can better appreciate and value how much those who came before us have left us. Perhaps not everything was good, but certainly not everything was bad either, so be grateful and remember that ancestral karma is less than 10 percent of our total karma.

Destiny Karma

Divine karma, or destiny karma, is the subtlest and one of the most important aspects of karma. It originates from the consciousness of the Higher Self and represents a kind of agreement made by the soul with the Divine before incarnation. Complex yet profound, it constitutes only 2 percent of total karma, but holds immense significance. This type of karma determines factors such as birth conditions—health, size, disabilities, congenital diseases, and physical attributes—as well as birthplace. Life differs significantly for individuals born in diverse environments, such as the Mongolian steppes, Saudi Arabia, central Africa, or Finland.

Destiny karma encompasses the manner of your birth—whether natural or complex—as well as the identities and energies of your parents. It is connected to your ancestral karma through your parents' lineage. Only from that perfect combination of mother and father could you have emerged as you did. Destiny karma also includes specific events, circumstances of great luck or enormous tragedy, and accidents. Notably, even a minor detail in these instances can dramatically alter the course of one's life.

Destiny karma also encompasses illnesses that can radically alter one's life and transform a person completely. Death, too, is part of destiny karma—the time and manner of our passing are predestined. It's essential to remember that destiny karma brings experiences of all kinds—good and bad—and that each arrives as a teacher.

Destiny karma can be challenging to comprehend. Consider dwarfism—from a judgmental perspective, it might seem a terrible affliction causing suffering, humiliation, and the thwarting of dreams. We might assume this is bad karma. Yet, in certain cultures and historical periods, unique physical or mental attributes were revered as divine gifts. Moreover, there have been times and individuals for whom dwarfism yielded positive outcomes.

We judge reality through our own limited perspective. Women who now appear overweight or obese would have embodied ideal beauty standards centuries ago. Pale skin was once a status symbol, while today many seek a tan for pleasure and aesthetic reasons.

With this, I want to emphasize that we shouldn't judge karma or destiny. We don't know if, behind a complex birth in a difficult country, a soul is being formed that will be strong, and will transform the world when they grow up. Nor can we say it's good karma to be born into a wealthy home in a First World nation. We know now that birth, the history of parents—which would be ancestral karma, and the first years of life have an influence on us, but we also know that human beings have a profound power to shape their own lives.

Before we delve into present karma, it's essential to understand that, according to karmic teachings, a bright aspect of your Higher Self agrees to the timing, manner, and lessons of your incarnation. Even the circumstances of your departure are predetermined. Upon birth, we forget these agreements, but deep within the soul, each of us shares responsibility for creating our destiny karma.

Present Karma

Let's now talk about present karma, which constitutes 90 percent or more of what happens to us. Present karma is what we build daily through our decisions or omissions, reinforced by loving intentions or misdirected by anger and envy. The purpose of present karma is to focus on generating the maximum amount of positive karma so that negative or painful experiences are less severe. If you've accumulated a hundred points of positive karma and made only ten points of mistakes, that ninety-point difference will benefit you. I am convinced of the importance of adding bright karma through acts of compassion, service, and help—acts that are rooted in love, consciousness, and a clear purpose of serving others to be complete.

To be very clear, divine karma makes up 2 percent of our karma, ancestral karma is 8 percent, and present karma 90 percent. This is why, no matter how difficult your ancestral and divine karmas are, your present karma can modify, reconstruct, or transform your overall karmas.

When you ask yourself, "When will I see the effects of my present karma? When can I touch the things I'm setting in motion today? How much and how quickly will these seeds I've sown grow or germinate?" the answer is: it depends. The outcome is influenced by the energy you've invested and your understanding and application of the Principle of Generation and resonance. Remember, some seeds, like bamboo, take years to sprout but then may grow ten feet tall in a single growing season. Others may germinate quickly but yield disappointing results. Ultimately, the timing and outcome of your actions can only be discovered through experience.

I want to tell you a story about present karma and how life takes its time to return those good things you have sown.

Many years ago, I was a therapist and saw thousands of people. I don't remember them all, but I do know that every day I sat in my office, I had the genuine and legitimate purpose of doing something good for their lives, of helping and supporting them.

One day, I myself experienced a deeply difficult situation, one of true despair. Believing all options were exhausted, I desperately needed a loan to overcome an urgent situation. So, I went to a pawn shop and was met with a very smiling and loving gaze. Unexpectedly, the person attending the establishment took me to an office and lent me the money without me having to leave anything in pawn. For me, the event was very surprising, so I asked, "Why did you do this?" And the woman replied, "You don't recognize me, but some time ago I went to your office. I didn't have money to pay you, and you said to me, 'Pay me what you can.' You accepted what I could give you, and the help you gave me at that time was invaluable to me. Things have gone well for me, and today I own this pawn shop. Take the loan, you don't have to sign any paperwork. I know when you have the money, you will come back."

I was disconcerted and didn't know what to do, but I said, "Yes, I have to receive." The good things we give are sown like seeds; when the fruits ripen, they must be received with joy. I returned a few weeks later to repay the entire loan. It was a tremendous gift and a valuable lesson. Though I didn't remember the woman, she remembered me and appeared in my life at the precise moment I needed her—that's how karma operates.

When awareness is limited, it's easy to confuse karma with luck. We observe others' experiences and mistakenly attribute their abundance to good fortune. Someone with an athletic physique, for example, is often perceived as having merely inherited or acquired it through some luck. We fail to recognize that behind all success lies an underlying energy.

Each of us is successful in what we have dedicated our time and attention to. It is very important to understand that karma is precious because it can be stored, because it is flexible, and because it is sown and emerges at the precise moment it needs to be.

Some people have good karma when it comes to abundance and will never lack anything, as if it were a prize. There are beings who possess divine karma with joy, who find it easy to be happy, who were born with a very healthy body from their divine karma. Others who, by family inheritance, received a business though ancestral karma and, with discipline and work, have made it grow.

It is very important to discover how the three karmas are related, how they connect and intertwine. A full and happy life is an effect, but also a cause. It's crucial for us to acknowledge that, to live the life we want to live, we must sow the best seeds.

Be very careful what you ask for, or when assuming life is unfair; instead, from the bottom of your heart, take responsibility for your actions. It's okay to look back and ask yourself what karma your ancestors have left you, and perhaps also to observe some of your attributes as divine karma, gifts given to you from the beginning of your life. But, above all, the most important thing is that you perceive what you are generating, what you are emitting, and how the seeds you sow will bear fruit at the right time.

Those who are serious about dharma . . . strive to remain consciously attentive.

NAROPA

Universal Law V

Principle of Dharma

Whoever sows light shall reap light;
this is how dharma works.

Right now, as I review this chapter, I am in India, still uncovering its magic and mysticism. It's easy to see how such profound philosophy could emerge from such a vibrant land. In a way, it's clear that only a world brimming with such rich spices could give birth to a consciousness as vast as the reality it seeks to understand.

There is an Indian proverb that says, "Watch your thoughts, for they become words. Watch your words, for they become actions. Watch your actions, for they become habits. Watch your habits, for they become your character. Watch your character, for it becomes your destiny."

By carefully examining this paragraph, we can infer that tending to our thoughts can lead to transformative changes in our habits.

Correcting thought patterns can positively influence our words and actions. Rather than focusing solely on rectifying external behaviors, we can delve deeper into our core beliefs and values. In this way, instead of focusing on pruning the tree once it has grown, we can anticipate and, from the very beginning, foster personal growth and create a beneficial impact on those around us.

Karma, simply put, is the culmination of thoughts, intentions, emotions, or consciousness we've sown. The more knowledge, attention, and love we give to that karma, the stronger and more vivid it will become. Therefore, we could say that dharma is the "positive" karma we generate.

Knowing that my actions could cause harm, yet doing them anyway, generates significant karmic consequences. If, in addition, I know I am causing harm and my purpose is to hurt someone, that will produce even more significant karmic consequences. It is important to understand that when you have more consciousness, more information, and more wisdom, you are a greater generator of karma. Thus, an adult who knows clearly what they are doing, when they harm a child for example, is producing immense karma.

The seeds I am sowing—which are nourished by intention and attention, by thought, charge, and consciousness—can be positive or negative. When we refer to positive, beneficial, and bright karma, we speak of dharma, which is the sowing of seeds that will end up generating a garden full of blessings.

WHAT IS DHARMA?

Dharma is a polysemic word—it has many meanings. In Hinduism and Buddhism dharma is defined as one's individual duty, a virtuous purpose—it can even be interpreted as a law of behavior with very defined doctrines; to do the right thing, to act in the best way we can, is to generate dharma.

It can also be understood as a guiding axis of life, as the possibility of constructing and co-creating an existence centered on the good things we do, knowing they will bring rewards, blessings, and benefits to our future story.

An oversimplified view of dharma would be to see it as good karma, but it encompasses a broader scope. Dharma is order, it is what is right; dharma, from a very conscious perspective, is the generation of actions that allow us to achieve self-fulfillment and that, by doing so in a beneficial way, also contribute to the growth of others. If we embody our dharma to the fullest, we cooperate with a greater good for the planet and all sentient or conscious beings.

When people commit harmful acts out of ignorance, it suggests a lack of understanding about life's purpose. But those who knowingly inflict harm on others generate destructive karma that will inevitably catch up with them.

As human consciousness evolves, we become more enlightened and wiser, naturally choosing actions that are right, meaningful, and beneficial to all. This is dharma.

Let's envision a forest, a space where every creature thrives. All trees possess the right to grow. Each seeks its own sunlight and arranges itself harmoniously with the others.

When you live well, without interfering with the growth of others, when you help and cooperate with others to evolve and improve, then you are living in order—you are living in dharma.

Dharma is related to the Principle of Oneness, which we read about at the beginning of this book, it is the opposite of separation. Dharma is contrary to rupture, violence, illness, and suffering.

To move toward dharma, we must rectify our thoughts and align ourselves with intention from the mind, with a purpose and with love in our heart. If we could detach ourselves from substantial ignorance, that is, from the inability to see things in their full dimension, if we could let go of the unconscious knowledge of our ego's desire, then we would live in a more dharmic way.

Hinduism teaches that at the center of all of us and all of creation there is light. Sometimes that light is covered by layers of pain, resentment, past wounds, or very particular life circumstances that may have hurt us and led us astray from the right path, in such a way that some human beings have lost the ability to see their own bright essence.

The call now is for you to be able to penetrate those superficial layers and allow the light to emerge. May your life, your actions, your thoughts, what you generate, and all that you resonate with be in perfect order and harmony. This is the beginning of a good life and a full, happy existence.

Do you remember how, in the Principle of Resonance, as similar elements converge, the collective energy they emit intensifies? Now imagine a hypothetical circumstance where ignorant people—and I'm not talking about academic ignorance, but ignorance of life, of the universe, of the laws, of the principles that govern order—come together. When someone disregards the fact that violence destroys and harms, they are more likely to cross paths with another person who also wants to generate violence. Then violence grows and expands, and between them they attract, through resonance, more and more circumstances in which to experience violence.

If someone hurts another willingly, with an underlying intention to cause suffering, that will bring about a negative resonance. Over time, sharing with so many people, I've discovered that most people don't want to hurt; it's not usually someone's desire to hurt their spouse with their words, for example, and yet they do.

Remember, there are many forces being emitted—your actions and your words, but also your intention and purpose. Karma is every seed you sow. Dharma is the seed that is coated in knowledge, wisdom, and love. Just as two violent beings come together to do harm, and their force is amplified, when two people unite in goodness, in an intention of service, cooperation, or helpfulness in a quest to live in a healthier and better way, this also resonates and amplifies.

Our capacity to harm obscures our true essence, that light that shines within. We must learn to cultivate a life grounded in compassion, love, and awareness, in order to naturally create a life aligned with dharma, yielding positive outcomes, harmonious experiences, supportive relationships, and profound joy.

Within spiritual knowledge, there are many secrets that remain unrevealed, jealously guarded under the notion that they should only be shared among initiates, among individuals who have dedicated a significant portion of their lives to the study and contemplation of the highest precepts. Today, I offer you one of these teachings from a dharmic perspective, for my purpose is that upon understanding it, you may apply it to your life, bringing blessings to you and those around you. The secret lies in the understanding that both karma and dharma originate from the same energy source. This energy can be channeled into sowing either bright seeds or destructive/neutral ones. The distinction lies in one's level of consciousness. A higher consciousness enables the choice of compassionate actions, while a lower consciousness often defaults to simpler, sometimes harmful choices.

Let me give you an example. Imagine yourself in a vast, unknown space. You're not aware of how you got there, but you traverse a series of caverns, finding yourself enveloped by immense emptiness. After exploring this grandeur in solitude, you look up to find darkness. Armed with a small torch, you cautiously progress, illuminating only a few feet ahead. Along the way, you discover hidden treasures. Suddenly, a blinding light erupts like a flash of lightning, and you can see for a moment that you're inside a very opulent place, full of jewels, treasures, books, and relics.

Everything around you is breathtaking, but then the brilliance fades and darkness returns. You're left with your small torch, trying to illuminate the space, but it's impossible because you can't encompass the majesty around you. Now you know that all those treasures and relics are there, all of that exists, but you don't know how to see it again. The moment was so brief, so fleeting, you can't retain all the information of what you saw.

This is very similar to spiritual awakening. This is what consciousness and the Principle of Dharma are about. Suddenly, the light reaches you, and you understand that you can do good in the world. You discover you are capable of generating simple or complex acts that bring the greatest good to everyone around you—and then something within you changes.

Today, I want to tell you that you have the power to consciously choose to perform dharmic actions. You can discern between doing something without any benefit and doing things with a purpose of helping, cooperating, serving, and contributing to a greater good. If you learn to choose between doing something in a simple way or putting love and a higher purpose into it, then you will be directly on the path of dharma, and that space filled with treasures will reveal itself to you with increasing clarity.

You can practice dharma through actions. Undoubtedly, caring for a sick person, giving loving advice to a friend, helping the poor, being a good son, a good father, a good husband, a good employer, being compassionate and having a sense of responsibility toward the Earth, taking care of your pets—these are all dharmic actions. You can also practice dharma by thinking beautiful and bright thoughts, praying for others, and blessing the world.

When faced with a terrible circumstance, such as war, if we fill our hearts with anger or resentment, this will influence the generation and resonance of everything we attract to ourselves, and, of course, our karma. Violence attracts violence, and anger causes our environment to become filled with more rage and fury.

During times of war, you can pray for peace, wish for the greater good, and refrain from taking sides, from falling into the temptation of judging, and from labeling people as good or evil. Simply wish for a just and harmonious order to be established for all. This is also dharma.

Sometimes we perform wonderful acts yet are unaware of their transcendent meaning. That is why I believe in the power of prayer. One can do a great deal of dharma from within the heart by asking the Higher Power for the greater good for all. You can practice dharma by accompanying your thoughts with a wish for someone who wants to improve or endure, wishing a business to prosper, a person to have a good journey, or a book like this to find the best paths to grow and flourish.

We generate dharma when we meditate, act with care for the planet, when we care for a tree or an animal, when we protect a vulnerable person, or help someone in need. We create dharma with our words when we support selflessly, silencing judgments or remaining quiet in the face of harmful comments toward others. Perhaps, faced with harmful comments you act as a brave defender of justice, thereby generating a greater good; but sometimes simply remaining silent and not contributing your own judgment is also a beneficial act. When you share a little of what you have without anyone knowing, when you teach what you know, when you assist someone you don't even know, you are generating dharma.

Dharma is wisdom and learning, prudence and respect. Dharma is thinking, living, and feeling what light you have to give to the world, and doing so with the best intention from your heart.

Let me give you an example regarding abundance. If you give abundantly, hoping for a heavenly reward or desiring others to see and applaud you, what would be the effect of the seed you are sowing? Are you truly acting from the desire to help or the desire for applause? Is it genuinely an act of sharing or do you want to earn a higher heaven for your "great generosity"? But if, on the contrary, from humility and silence you give discreetly, moved only by the intention to help without expecting rewards or desiring applause and solely with the simplicity of your heart, then the purpose will have a different seed, and life, I am sure, will reward you with beautiful and bright things.

Simply with your words, glances, and thoughts, you can influence someone else's dharma or karma. When an acquaintance tells you they are about to start a business and you say, "You're going to do very poorly," you are sowing a destructive seed, a harmful karma. But if you wish them well, if you light a candle or, from the depths of your heart, pray to the Higher Power for that person's well-being, then you will be sowing a precious dharma for yourself and for them, which will perhaps bring benefits to those you love most, when they need it most.

If someone close to you aspires to be an artist, offering support rather than criticism cultivates positive dharma. By expressing belief in their abilities, dreams, and potential for success, you empower them and contribute to their journey, activating a good dharma.

It is crucial to recognize that our impact extends beyond overt actions and words. Subtle cues, like disapproving or trusting glances, even unspoken thoughts, carry significant weight. Affirmations such as "I believe/trust/decree/influence/align for your success" exemplify dharmic action through supportive intentions for others.

So, the next time you find yourself in a negative attitude and wishing ill on someone, remember that you are creating karma. Also, be aware that you can modify your attitude. Simply connect with yourself, shift your focus, and emit something that is productive, beneficial, and good for others.

If you can't do it, if within you there is simply no capacity to wish for good, then at least wish for nothing. It is much better for your karma to be neutral than negative and destructive. Remember, what you emit will come back to you.

At the beginning of this chapter, I shared a Hindu proverb I will now revisit to show you can make a destiny dharma; you can transform your future if you learn this lesson.

Your destiny stems from your character, your character from your habits, your habits from your actions, and your actions from your words. Words come from your thoughts and, I would add, "from the light of your heart." So, where does the change of destiny begin? With a job change? With a new house? The answer is no. I invite you to understand that dharma originates in your heart and mind, from there it passes to your words, actions, habits, and character. And it is here that your destiny is shaped.

Therefore, if you want to modify your reality in a consistently positive and bright way, you must remember that your destiny, the bright seeds you intend to see blossom in the future, begin now in your heart. Dharmic thoughts—those aligned with the highest good for yourself and others—are seeds of positive change.

They embody benevolence and a commitment to the collective well-being.

Dharmic thoughts will be reflected in dharmic words. These are words with a special energy when applied coherently. Although we are talking about dharma, you have to examine how it intertwines with the Principle of Generation and the Principle of Resonance, and how it vibrates in the Great Network that is the Principle of Oneness.

Some wonderful words that, when used from the heart, generate dharma are: "thank you," "I forgive you," "help me," "I help you," "I feel compassion for you," "I value your friendship," "I commit myself," "I do it for love," and "I free you and I free myself."

Incorporating powerful words into our vocabulary can transform our thoughts, leading to positive changes in our lives. By expanding our consciousness, we can cultivate a healthier, more fulfilling existence. Change takes time, but you can start cultivating it today.

By aligning with your dharma, I create dharma for myself.

Three Dharmic Insights

I offer three profound insights for your consideration, to be gradually incorporated into your life. Remember, spirituality's essence lies not in intellectual understanding or reading about it in books, but in heartfelt embodiment and expressed action.

- *The foundational insight declares: "Only good is real."*

Within oneness, a governing philosophy exists—goodness. Thus, in the Great Network, only good is authentic. Through the Principle of Generation, I cultivate goodness, and in doing so I align with positive forces. Through the Principle of Resonance, I attract good things.

By sowing beneficial seeds, or karma, I cultivate dharma, a path of righteousness. Repeating "Only good is real" integrates the five principles we've explored.

- *The second insight teaches us that "The central source of the universe loves me."*

When I think of love from the center of the Great Network, I am connecting with generation and resonance, but also with the dharmic energy that will undoubtedly bring more love into my life. Moreover, I can understand, according to the Principle of Oneness, that the central source is everywhere at the same time because we are part of a vibrant, pulsating Great Network of information.

- *The third insight states "Life flows in my favor."*

This assertion acknowledges life as the generative foundation of all things, moving through the universe and benefiting us when rooted in positive intentions, purposes, and wishes. Recall our discussion on the significance of intention, purpose, and heartfelt love in resonance and creation. These three dharmic insights, when aligned through conscious repetition and heartfelt love, produce beneficial outcomes.

REFLECTING ON KARMA AND DHARMA

In the previous chapter, we explored the concept of karma, which revealed how our actions—like sown seeds—produce corresponding results. This chapter introduced dharma, which emphasizes cultivating beneficial actions to yield positive outcomes. While karma focuses on personal responsibility for cause and effect, dharma encourages a broader perspective of contributing to the collective good and being receptive to its rewards.

Karma focuses on looking back at past causes that have resulted in our present, but dharma tells us to be aware of the good things we do now, in the present, to continue attracting good things into our lives. And if at any time we have done "bad" deeds, dharma tells us to immediately generate "good" deeds to correct our path and receive the best results.

Self-Reflection

I propose a reflective exercise. I invite you to ask yourself how much good you are bringing into the world in your daily tasks, if your presence adds value and contributes to the people around you today.

- *How much dharma have you generated today?*

Don't be too harsh or strict with yourself. Perhaps you called your mother and made her day, or maybe you helped your children put on their shoes and made their lives easier, perhaps you spent time with a friend in the morning, or were empathetic with someone you encountered on the street, or perhaps you were patient with someone. Dharma is not always in the big, shining actions, it is also subtly hidden in small acts, in accompanying with affection, in caring responsibly, in doing our daily work with care, or in being good people promoting a greater good.

- *Reflect on the karma you've cultivated over time.*

Consider the people who've enriched your life with knowledge, health, harmony, and peace. Express gratitude to your parents, grandparents, caretakers, siblings, friends, and mentors for their belief in you. By acknowledging their contributions, you amplify their dharma, celebrating the fruition of their positive actions. Simultaneously, your humility and self-awareness deepen your own spiritual growth.

In dharma, as in many other energetic movements in life, the more emotion, intention, consciousness, and presence we put in, the more energy will accompany us. This is not only about generating dharma in words but also in emotions, being coherent, influencing purpose and intention, wishing with all our heart that things go well for us and others, making the actions we generate day by day arise from deep within us, with light and a true intention to be good to ourselves, to be good to others, and to improve the world.

Our dharma should be aligned in thought, mind, and intention, allowing our heart to radiate expansive energy. You might at this moment feel the presence of the Great Network—that is oneness—and from there generate the desire that things go very well for you—that is generation. Simultaneously extend goodwill to others, envisioning their success and abundance. Attract beneficial circumstances, allies, and lessons by connecting with this collective energy—this is resonance.

Moreover, understand that when you sow seeds from a beautiful place—that's karma. And these seeds, in coherence and love, are coated in love and good intentions for yourself and others. If this light you nourish leads to good things happening to you, your family, your community, and the entire world, you're generating dharma. Now you understand that all these principles are intertwined.

REFLECTION: SOWING SEEDS FOR YOUR FUTURE

When you're older, you'll have a tree in the center of your inner garden. Perhaps the fruits of the tree will be sweet and pleasant, like honey and sugar, companionship and sweetness, nourishment and blessings. Or perhaps they will be bitter and sour, like solitude and pain, sickness and chaos, fear and anguish, debt and abandonment. You have to be aware that you alone have cultivated this tree through every action, every thought, every book you read, every song you listened to, every opportunity you had to help or cooperate with someone else.

Now, imagine that today—right now—you are sowing the seeds of your future, the seeds of your health, your mental clarity, your emotional balance, and your personal relationships—you are sowing your destiny.

Sow abundantly with love and dharma, nurturing bright seeds so that at the end of your story, and every day from now on, you can reap beautiful fruits that bring joy, peace, and fulfillment to the life you're living.

Never expect, never assume, never ask,
and never demand. Let things happen.
If something is meant to be, it will be.

ANONYMOUS

Universal Law VI

Principle of Wu Wei

Wu wei, which means "action through inaction," is the art of letting life happen, of understanding the perfect flow of events.

Historically, spiritual traditions often required a form of exchange to fully reveal their depth and meaning. This exchange served as a demonstration of a student's commitment, willingness, and attitude toward receiving teachings. While today we primarily use money to acquire goods, many invaluable assets—intangible in nature—transcend monetary value. Sacred teachings, the ability to heal others, interspecies contact, or the possibility of entering the subtle planes of existence cannot be paid for with money alone.

In ancient times, spiritual traditions demanded specific forms of payment known as "initiations." These exchanges of consciousness, energy, intention, and focus served as assessments of a student's readiness for deeper knowledge.

Some spiritual paths demanded rites of strength, trials such as labyrinths, even exceptional journeys. Among these schools of knowledge and the tolls or fees they charged their initiates, there is one that particularly catches my attention. Aspiring students of a great school of wisdom on the islands of the Aegean Sea were required to row a small boat alone for three days, their provisions limited to food and water. Afterward, they relinquished their oars, trusting the tides to carry them to shore, where higher knowledge awaited. This might seem absurd to our information-saturated minds, yet ancient people understood it as a test of trust in the universe's rhythms.

Until now, our paradigms and beliefs about spirituality and human growth dictate in most cases that it is our responsibility to apply the Principle of Generation to its fullest extent, that most of the experiences we live depend 100 percent on us and our free will. This is true, as we learned it in the first, second, and third chapters; however, I want to give you a look at spirituality from the East, from distant China, understanding that the universe is also very wise and that there are reasons things happen as they do.

This principle changed my life profoundly. After I discovered it, I dedicated a whole year of my spiritual growth entirely to working on it. I am referring to *wu wei*, which I started applying every day in many different circumstances, although it was initially challenging as it contradicted many familiar notions.

Our material world resists this principle. Ego is constantly immersed in the idea of struggle and judgment, and this Taoist view of the world is a latent threat to control, rigidity, and the mind's reason-centered thinking.

Wu wei is a very special way of seeing the world, a harmonious way of approaching life. Each human society develops its own philosophy, culture, and worldview. These cultural frameworks are shaped by geographical location, lifestyle, and activities.

It's easy to understand why Norse gods are often depicted as strong men. Their battles against giant wolves and sea storms demand physical prowess. Living in Norwegian or Swedish fjords, they likely developed light eyes and hardy constitutions in order to withstand the region's harsh climate, including long, dark winters. Conquering stormy seas further shaped their image as powerful, imposing figures.

Caribbean deities are often envisioned as sensual, luminous women associated with beauty and fertility. These divine artisans and dancers are embodiments of joy. Unlike Norse gods, they do not fight wolves. They focus on cultivating harmony and manipulating forces to ensure bountiful harvests. The region's idyllic climate and breathtaking landscapes foster a celebration of light, ocean, and life's abundance.

Desert environments, like the Sahara and Atacama, do not foster the worship of exuberant, robust deities. The harsh conditions demand different divine figures. Instead of bountiful gods, these cultures revere those associated with the sun, chaos, and moisture—powers essential for sustaining life in such barren landscapes.

The Judeo-Christian tradition emerged from cultures shaped by scarcity and relentless struggle. Desert environments necessitated the protection of limited resources. These societies developed survival strategies within powerful empires. Consequently, Judeo-Christian heritage emphasizes striving, self-defense, sacrifice, and a belief in a stern deity, mirroring the harsh desert sun.

Therefore, if you grew up in a society with Judeo-Christian

influence, it is implied that you must fight, protect, and defend life; that you must traverse inner deserts; that your consciousness must be associated with the precepts of survival and compassion, but also, positively, with generosity among caravans, sharing the precepts of staying together as a community to overcome difficulties.

However, the Principle of Wu Wei arises from a very different worldview, from another culture where struggle is not predominant. In the philosophy of wu wei, which originated in ancient China, spiritual values are associated with a gentle and docile nature, with great rivers and precious waterfalls; its values are based on the flow, progress, and generosity of life.

Remember that the Chinese people are deeply rooted in their traditions. In some communities, they continue to preserve ancient doctrinal practices, venerating the wisdom of their ancestors.

One of the most influential philosophers in Chinese culture is Lao Tzu, traditionally credited with authoring the *Tao Te Ching* (also known as the *Tao Te King*). This renowned text encapsulates many of the Tao path's core teachings. Within the path of Tao lies the Principle of Wu Wei.

LAO TZU

Founders of spiritual traditions often embody the wisdom they teach. Lao Tzu's life is a remarkable example, which we'll briefly explore.

Lao Tzu, a revered sage and perhaps the most influential thinker of his era, served as an official in the imperial library. Contrary to the modern concept of a librarian, he was a custodian of sacred knowledge, responsible for its preservation, organization, and protection. As an elder scholar, Lao Tzu possessed the keys to the era's greatest wisdom.

Lao Tzu had been a faithful servant of the Imperial House, but one day he decided he had to free himself from his bonds and embark on a quest for inner wisdom. But no one would allow a sage of that nature to simply leave the palace, so he was ordered to remain there.

Legend has it that Lao Tzu had no choice but to depart on a water buffalo, a mythical creature that symbolizes the Tao. These large, docile animals are often found submerged in muddy rice paddies. During a trip to Vietnam, I had the opportunity to observe these magnificent creatures firsthand. The choice of a water buffalo as Lao Tzu's mount is deeply symbolic. In contrast to the swiftness of horses or carriages, the water buffalo is slow and heavy, yet large and humble. Its simplicity belies its power, mirroring the essence of the Tao itself.

Knowing that no one could leave the empire without passing through its gates, the emperor let Lao Tzu go, but secretly dispatched a messenger to prevent his departure.

Days later, upon reaching the border, Lao Tzu encountered a guard who forbade his passage, citing a direct order from the sovereign. With compassion, Lao Tzu pleaded for release, expressing a desire to experience true freedom and life beyond his familiar world. He said that he had learned a great deal and that it was time to share the wisdom he had gained. The guard remained steadfast, and Lao Tzu awaited his fate. But it is said that the guard's resolve suddenly softened, and he proposed a compromise: "If you can commit all your knowledge to writing, the emperor cannot punish me for your departure."

According to the legend, Lao Tzu sat down to write, and spent an entire night formulating one of the most beautiful books of knowledge of all time—the *Tao Te Ching*. It is said that, in one night, he wrote these universal precepts in an uninterrupted flow that continues to amaze all those who delve into the search for his great knowledge. When Lao Tzu delivered the book, the guard was fascinated, convinced that, having taken the information from the sage, the emperor would not care about an old decrepit man riding a water buffalo. Thus, Lao Tzu left the Chinese border and was lost in the eternity of time and the infinity of the valleys, beyond the known world.

I feel a profound connection with Lao Tzu. His life and teachings resonate deeply with my soul. Renouncing wealth and power, this sage sought freedom, embarking on a journey accompanied only by a water buffalo.

He offers numerous teachings, but one stands out—we can spend a lifetime acquiring knowledge and building wisdom, yet true understanding comes from experience. Only when wisdom is fully integrated into life can we aspire to enlightenment.

THE TAO

For our Western philosophy, overly entrenched since the Industrial Revolution and scientific thought, it is difficult to comprehend Tao and its characteristics. Tao means "way." It is the way of totality, unity, and understanding the essence of things.

In the Western worldview, we demand that the earth yield five, six, or even seven harvests annually. We force lettuce to grow in greenhouses, treating them like machines, and deceive hens into laying more eggs by subjecting them to artificial light. Such practices are aberrant.

We impose hyper-early stimulation on children from the moment they are conceived, and by the age of two they already know a lot of things, but they haven't matured in their essential part.

All this acceleration is gradually leading us to force the rhythms and times of life, to have younger and younger adolescents and adults who do not manage to mature even at forty or fifty years old.

Our technologically "advanced" society is paradoxically fraught with anxiety and stress. Taoism offers a counterpoint: "No matter how hard the farmer pulls the carrot; it won't grow faster." This adage encapsulates our modern impatience—demanding accelerated maturity from children, rapid muscle growth in our bodies, instant business success, and accelerated spiritual enlightenment.

Despite our best efforts and attempts to control outcomes, we consistently find ourselves at the mercy of natural processes and cycles. The Tao teaches that everything requires time to mature—a carrot to grow, a woman to develop, a man to evolve, and love to flourish.

The Tao also teaches us, among many other wonders, the Principle of Wu Wei, which states that living with difficulty prevents us from valuing life, while living with simplicity and acceptance leads us to appreciate life.

Consider this: how many difficulties are there in your life? And of these, how many have you created yourself? How many things that are not problems do we turn into problems? How many experiences that are not conflicts do we lead to become a conflict? So, it's not just about living with difficulty but becoming attached to difficulty, becoming addicted to problems, not being able to live without stress or without creating unpleasant experiences.

Go deeper and give yourself the opportunity to review these questions and analyze yourself while doing so. Question yourself honestly: How addicted are you to conflict? How accustomed are you to shouting, fighting, getting angry about the same things that have no solution? It is your self-responsibility to observe yourself without judging. How much do you like, and how accustomed are you to focusing on, judgment, criticism, and your own mistakes or those of others?

Have you noticed the overwhelming negativity in newscasts and mass media? Positive news is rare because it lacks the appeal of conflict and drama. We are drawn to sensational stories of violence, conflict, blood, and death. We are, little by little and without realizing it, resonating more and more with violence and tragedies than with peace and inner serenity.

Given this, it's worth considering: What are we truly doing with our lives? From childhood, we're inundated with conflict, violence, drama, and tragedy. We learn that relationships are battlegrounds, abundance requires struggle, and success is paramount. Worse yet, we perpetuate these harmful patterns. How many of these fighting habits do you teach and pass on to those around you? How often do you open your children's bedroom door and hope it's messy so you can yell at them in the morning? How often do you impatiently look at the clock, wishing your client or partner would be three minutes late so you can start a fight? Meals become battles, and road rage is a common reflex. How long can we sustain peace amidst constant conflict and turmoil?

We have so many habits of struggle, of chaos, of fighting, that perhaps we don't see them. They have become so close to us, they are part of our unconscious. The habit of conflict is not just about shouting and throwing tantrums; there are people who are silent yet carry a battle within. There are very quiet people who practice passive violence, those who say nothing but who are living an internal catastrophe. Some smile, are sweet and polite, but their minds are full of the most terrible thoughts. We need to learn to evaluate ourselves because, as long as we don't take charge of that, we will continue to repeat and live in a world marked by conflict.

In a clarifying way, I want you to ask yourself: If there is conflict in my mind, what am I going to generate? If there is rage in my heart, what will I resonate with? If most of my actions are wrapped up in struggle, what kind of karma will I sow?

Universal Laws serve to guide us toward what we do want to experience, but also to move us away from what we don't want to continue doing.

Whether planning a trip, a business meeting, or a casual encounter, some people fill their minds with anxious thoughts: What if the food is terrible? Will people like me? Might someone take advantage of me? Should I prepare for a confrontation? Unbeknownst to them, they're stockpiling potential conflicts, inviting negative experiences.

Conversely, others embrace dharma proactively, affirming, "Let joy prevail. May all beings flourish. May the greater good unfold." This approach yields a radically different experience. Life's richness is often obscured by challenges. Constant adversity limits our perspective.

In every message, network transmission, lecture, or retreat, I emphasize the importance of appreciating simple pleasures—the light, the afternoon, a flower, the sky, and tranquility. Many dismiss this, saying, "What a drag, how boring. I already know about that." Yet, few can truly break free from habitual complaining and conflict to embrace consciousness, generation, resonance, and dharma of beauty, gratitude, and the present moment.

To fully grasp a philosophy and its underlying worldview and cosmology, immersing oneself in its origins is essential. I am profoundly grateful to have had the opportunity to explore Buddhism in Nepal, India, Tibet, Thailand, and Myanmar; to experience Zen in Japan's temples; and to encounter the legacy of Ancient Egypt in its temples and pyramids.

I was fortunate to discover Taoism in Vietnam, a nation where the Tao is perhaps more vibrant than anywhere else. Beyond the philosophical aspects, I experienced the Tao through the living world—sitting by cascading waterfalls, vast rice paddies, and lotus-filled lakes; observing the farmers and witnessing the miracle of rice cultivation. Meditating in Vietnam, I grasped the spirit of the Tao. The submerged rice fields were particularly revelatory. They are flooded using an awe-inspiring technique, and then, without human intervention, the earth gradually absorbs the water, day by day, with perfect timing. This natural cycle, I realized, mirrored the Tao's path—allowing things to unfold, trusting in the universe's innate ability to create, doing one's part, and then letting nature complete the work. With wet feet and eyes filled with beauty, I experienced Tao firsthand—not through words or teachers. Only Tao, all Tao, one with Tao.

The Tao, or "the Way," is often described as ineffable; it dwells in silence, transcending language and thought. Nature serves as a profound wellspring of Taoist wisdom. In nature, we find Taoist precepts—order, rhythm, peace, cooperation, flow. A walk in the woods, a sail across the ocean, or a hike through the hills reveals these essential truths. Everything that exists in nature spontaneously and essentially is Tao, and our life should, according to this view, focus on learning from nature.

This raises a question: If nature contains so much wisdom, why do hurricanes, earthquakes, storms, and natural disasters occur? Well, although it may seem difficult to understand, this apparent chaos is necessary and part of life. It obeys a higher order, a Principle of Oneness. Hurricanes and earthquakes have rhythms, although we cannot see them, and they follow structured and harmonious patterns, even though, from our perception, they are destructive. Nature has contrasts.

Just as there are flowers, so too is there volcanic lava; just as there are cute and cuddly animals, so too are there fierce predators. A lion preys on zebras, a shark devours small fish—this is also nature. Nature is not just a field of violet flowers, it can also be the devastation of a wildfire. Yet, complex as it may seem, there is an underlying order, and there is no conflict. There is complete coherence in the sky when it rains, in the falling snow, in the moving ocean, and in the blowing winds.

Even if a gale comes and is about to tear the branches from a tree, the tree does not complain, saying, "How unfair that the wind blows only upon me." Nor does the wind, with ego, say, "I will seize that tree and destroy it." For conflict to exist, there must be ego. Nature transcends this, embodying a consciousness of oneness. This is why there is no conflict within nature.

The Principle of Wu Wei is, undoubtedly, a teaching of higher spirituality that shows us how to live in simplicity and acceptance, renouncing struggle, attachment, and conflict.

"Wu wei" does not have a perfect translation into English but, as I have been able to understand, it refers to: "Let things happen without resisting."

Thus, the sun begins its daily journey across the sky, plants grow without anyone stretching them, the winds blow without anyone hurrying them from behind with a clock. Tao is forceful against our arrogant vision. We presume that lettuce requires precise temperature control to thrive, yet Tao counters, "Have not wild lettuce varieties flourished for millennia without human cultivation? Your arrogance and ego inflate your sense of importance in their growth."

The wind blows freely, unconstrained. And we say, "Hey, I'm going to build a system to block it or redirect it as I want." The Tao, however, questions this audacity: "How can you command the wind? It predates you and will persist regardless of your efforts." Water, too, has flowed independently, since before we even existed, and will continue to flow long after we are gone, because the universe, nature, and life are greater than our acts of immense arrogance.

According to wu wei, we must relinquish battles, efforts, and struggle. When we embrace this resonance, we foster a harmonious flow, aligning personal desires with the cosmic will. This dynamic replaces conflict with a dance of cooperation.

Wu wei emphasizes the value of learning to co-create with life, and the value of learning that your intention and the universe's intention become one. In the Principle of Generation, the energy is yours—you generate it for something to happen. In wu wei, you barely put in an effort, and trust that the universe will do the rest. Wu wei is the association of your desire with the great universal desire, a deep connection between your spirit and the universal spirit.

We can say that, typically, our minds operate independently. However, wu wei introduces us to a creative collective consciousness. This means that, rather than relying on ego, we connect with a Higher Power through prayer, offering, and humility. This shift transforms us from arrogant individuals into receptive channels for life's flow—you'll realize that life goes on; you'll believe the forces of the universe can work in your favor. Your being will remember it is part of oneness, of totality, of the whole.

Let's take a moment for some self-reflection. How often have you turned down great opportunities life has presented to you? I'm talking about preconceived biases like:

I would never date a short guy.
I would never get a loan.
I swear I'll never visit that country.
No matter what, I'm not studying Chinese.

How often do we arrogantly assume we know better than the universe? And yet, time and time again, we've ended up dating that short guy, taking out that loan, visiting that unexpected country—and having a fantastic time.

Wu wei suggests that, instead of striving to control your life, you should adopt a more receptive attitude in order to allow the universe to act in your favor. Now, ask yourself: How often have I resisted a new book, course, or adventure, only to discover later that it was an incredible experience? How many times have I turned down an opportunity, unaware that it could have been a transformative gift? Perhaps you've closed yourself off to knowledge and wisdom only to realize, upon opening up to it, that you've missed out on profound experiences and valuable insights you would not have otherwise achieved.

Imagine trees as great masters of Tao, they are truly impressive. They grow and nourish themselves from the earth, generously creating space for all to reach the sunlight. They even twist their branches to catch the vital rays of father sun.

Big trees make room for the little ones to grow. They don't compete with each other or fight against the changing seasons. Instead, they understand that we are all part of a larger whole. The old tree eventually makes way for the young, which in turn respects the wisdom of its predecessor, finding its own place in the world.

Trees communicate, dance, and flow. When a strong wind comes to strip them of their leaves, they simply let go. They don't resist. And when it's time for lush growth and bountiful harvests, they embrace the process fully, dropping their fruit.

Humans, however, tend to fight against anything different. We judge, we debate, and we create divisions when we feel threatened by competition. We cling too tightly to what we perceive as "ours," as if there were a clear boundary between our possessions and those of others. We rarely consider the collective "ours."

Our perspective is often incredibly self-centered, whether focused on individuals, races, or species:

> We English speakers are superior.
> We Jehovah's Witnesses have the one true faith.
> We tall people are more capable.
> We engineers are the smartest.

This divisive way of thinking undermines the Principle of Oneness.

I present to you one of the most profound questions from this book: How would your life change if you could simply *let go*?

It's natural to feel a bit scared by this. We've been conditioned to be efficient and in control, always striving to achieve more. We've been taught to compare ourselves to others and to feel inadequate when we don't measure up. We've been told that life is a constant struggle, a competition where only the strong survive.

We constantly find ourselves in battles—whether for winning a race, buying a faster car, creating a more defined six-pack, or striving for spiritual perfection. A lot of inner battles are constantly going through our heads.

We have come to believe that life and history are inherently conflictual. That progress requires sacrifice. That the world is divided into good and evil. That we need to defeat others to impose our ideals. This does not have to be so. Perhaps life imposes challenges, complex circumstances, but that does not mean we have to solve everything in conflict and struggle. Wu wei teaches us that life can be flow, it can be a synchronous movement, and that we can trust in letting go and allowing Great Wisdom to act.

I'm sure something inside you resonates with the possibility of sometimes embracing the Principle of Generation, and in other circumstances letting the inexhaustible flow and perfect movement act for you.

I also understand that your ego might resist this idea. The old part of you that craves control may be afraid of losing its grip. I invite you to consider these reflexive questions: How many times have you thought something was absolutely devastating? That a divorce would ruin your life, you'd never find a job as good, or that you'd never love again after so much pain.

Have you ever thought that what you were going through was the worst thing that could possibly happen? That it was the end of the road and there was no hope? And yet, things worked out and flowed, didn't they?

How many of those difficult experiences turned out to be valuable lessons or unexpected blessings?

You can see how our plans, our childhood dreams, and our illusion of control are all driven by our ego. Imagine war refugees or those fleeing conflict, losing their homes and possessions overnight and having to go wherever the wind takes them, not where they choose. I am sure many would have had thirty or forty better plans than boarding that train, that plane, or that ship to an unknown country. They were afraid, their lives changed—but they did it. Many found themselves in incredible places where they were able to start over and achieve things they never thought possible. And many migrants found a light and a strength they would never have seen in the place they came from.

There are people who are terrified of the mere thought that their children will not fulfill the plans they have designed for them and, yet, sometimes their children follow their own path and manage to have an extraordinary life. Consider this example from my own life: I never wanted my son to move abroad, but he did, married a wonderful woman, and gave me a grandson I adore. He has a better life than I could have imagined, partly because he didn't let me control his life.

We must learn to loosen our grip and realize we aren't always as wise as we think. There's something greater at play, and we can open ourselves to possibilities we never imagined.

Wu wei is not laziness. It doesn't mean becoming a couch potato, letting life do whatever it pleases. Wu wei isn't about disorder or neglect, nor is it about lounging in a hammock. Wu wei is about understanding that sometimes we need to act, while other times the best course of action is to do nothing at all.

If, for instance, a job opportunity comes your way, do everything you can to secure it—send your resume, attend the interview, prepare. But once you've done your part, let it go.

If you're longing for a trip, plan it and search for tickets. But if they're unavailable, just let it go. Sometimes the tickets will appear, and other times doors will open when you least expect it or stop insisting. You might wonder, "How can they open if I don't keep pushing?" This is the ego talking. Sometimes they open because there's an infinitely vast universe working on your behalf. The universe often knows the best path for us, and our impulses or ignorance can hinder the fulfillment of the Cosmic Mind's grand plan.

Sometimes wonderful things happen to us but we reject them because we misjudge them and rebel against them. I'm sure you've bought books on a whim and let them gather dust on a shelf. Then, years later, you open one and find the perfect answer you've been seeking, even though you acquired the book four or five years ago. It is at that moment that everything starts making sense and you realize the message was there all along, waiting for you.

The same thing happens to us in life. Sometimes we have the wrong perception of an injustice. However, perhaps that apparent injustice was a gift, a blessing, or was sustained by a greater plan.

I've heard countless people say, "I fought for my marriage despite the injustice." Yet, often, by letting go of that relationship, you may open yourself up to a brighter future. One that is happier and more fulfilling than the one you endured for so long.

The challenge lies in our inability to see the bigger picture. The universe often has greater plans for us, and letting go is sometimes the hardest yet most necessary step.

There's a remarkable wu wei tale about letting go. In a Brazilian town, almost every man worked at the local mine, and everyone clung to their job because there were apparently no other jobs. Year after year, despite suffering pain, injustice, low wages, abuse, illness, and even the death of their peers, the miners were so afraid of losing their jobs, they fought and clung to them no matter the harsh conditions. When someone was fired, there was crying and begging—they resisted being let go.

But one day when a miner was laid off, he did something unexpected. Instead of fighting the inevitable, he accepted it. With his severance pay, he started a small business. Each day, he traveled to a nearby city, bought hardware supplies—nails, hammers, chisels, plugs, and paints—and sold them back in his hometown. Gradually, his little business grew until he opened his own hardware store.

Time went by and his business grew even more. After a decade, this former miner was a wealthy man—not only in his town but also in his province. He no longer traveled to a nearby city, but imported the supplies. One day, he was asked the secret to his success. "Was it persistence? A lucky break? Did you have an extraordinary contact or a great business vision?" His reply was simple, "I just accepted my dismissal from the mine when it was time, and moved on. If I had fought to remain in my comfort zone, I would undoubtedly have continued to be a miner, like the rest of my companions, or lamented not being one."

Had those who migrated stayed in their hometown, had those women who entered the workforce persisted in their old notion of dependency, had countries clung to the old empires, had orphans remained trapped in their pain, none of them would be who they are today.

Beneath the surface of misfortune, injustice, and struggle, there lies a possibility of acceptance that counters the distorted perceptions fueled by ignorance. It's crucial to understand that acceptance can be a source of great strength, intelligence, and even grandeur. In accepting life's flow, there is immense power. Sometimes, simply letting life unfold is far more powerful than striving and fighting for what we think we want or believe life should be.

I've always been different. It was clear to me from a young age that I didn't fit in. I was bullied throughout my childhood and teen years, and even into college. It was a painful experience. I cried and I tried to defend myself by fighting back. I desperately tried to belong. But the more I tried to fit in, the more I was rejected. Eventually, I accepted my isolation and retreated into myself. I spent a lot of time alone, observing others and reflecting on my experiences. This solitude led me to meditation. Finding no one to talk or play with, I started exploring my inner world. From a young age, I became acutely aware of human behavior and the pain we inflict on each other. It was a difficult journey, but I developed a deep sense of compassion.

Early in my life, I struggled immensely, always trying to cover my "weirdness," to seem normal, continually going to great lengths to either defend who I was or doing everything I could to belong to an environment that simply did not accept me. But when I finally found clarity and embraced my individuality, everything changed—invaluable insights started coming my way. I met a few wonderful people. That bullied child, who learned empathy, compassion, and a quiet strength, is the reason I'm here today. By holding onto my desire to belong while simultaneously fighting for acceptance of who I am, I've transformed into the person I am today. I couldn't be writing this book or sharing these spiritual lessons without those difficult experiences. They were painful at the time, but they've served as rich fertilizer, allowing me to grow and thrive.

Wu wei teaches us mindfulness, showing us that sometimes after the struggle only a conscious, effortless, and fluid act remains. It shows us that sometimes we don't need the struggle, but simply to let go and release. When we truly understand wu wei, we naturally yearn for a fluid and more simple life, a harmonious journey in tune with ourselves and the universe.

Wu wei makes us see that life is a cosmic dance and not an imposition of egos, that we can let go and watch in amazement as life is also flowing in our favor. It teaches us that, rather than swimming upstream, we can go with the extraordinary flow of the waters and reach the great calm ocean, in acceptance and peace.

You decide if you want to continue believing that life is

struggle, fighting with everything and against everyone, or if you prefer that wu wei illuminates your consciousness and your heart, and you understand that perhaps, just perhaps, life is also about acceptance and flow.

Meditation for Letting Go

Please, close your eyes and meditate on what is happening now with your life.

Consider your present challenges. Who or what is causing you the most stress this week? What conflict has been dominating your month?

For a limited mind, all conflicts are justified. Cross that limit and allow yourself to enter a purer, more natural, more tranquil state.

Inhale and exhale slowly, relax your body, breathe calmly, and observe your life from a different perspective.

Imagine your life without struggles or conflicts. Step back a little and look at your life as if through a window. Observe from a distance your conflicts, battles, and the same old problems. Notice how they often repeat themselves, merely changing in form. What if these challenges, these perceived tragedies, are actually part of life's journey? What if that difficult situation or the forgiveness you struggle to give is simply a step toward greater happiness?

Breathe, release your fears, let go of the need to control, and simply flow.

See with clarity. Sometimes we perceive conflicts where there are none, or create struggles that don't exist. Sometimes we imagine enemies that vanish as soon as we shift our perspective and consciousness.

I'm going to rephrase a few questions for you, and I want you to ponder them. Let them flow through you.

The questions are: What if I ceased fighting? What if I stopped struggling? What if I simply let life unfold?

Look through the window again and choose one of your smallest battles. Tell one of those many conflicts, one of those struggles, "I release you."

Now imagine for a moment if, instead of living in conflict, you allowed yourself the gift of peace. How would it feel to simply let go? It's a possibility.

Take five slow, deep breaths, allowing your breath to flow naturally. Breathe simply because you can. Now take a couple of gentler breaths, then open your eyes as you exhale.

Everything flows, out and in;
everything has its tides; all things rise and fall;
the pendulum-swing manifests in everything.

THE KYBALION

Universal Law VII

Principle of Ollin

We must learn to find motion within stillness,
allowing our desires to align with the universe and
guide us toward the light, to flow with it.

Each one of the chapters you have read so far has shown you a different way of conceiving of and standing in the world. Most of the principles complement each other, and each one offers us the tools necessary to live in this unified universe, generating the best pulsations, resonating with the most harmonious possibilities, understanding karma and taking responsibility for the seeds we sow, cultivating a straight path that brings only dharmic blessings, and, finally, taking a step toward evolution, understanding that sometimes it is necessary to let go and let wu wei flow into our lives.

In this chapter, we'll delve into a principle from the spiritual tradition closest to my heart—shamanism—which describes *ollin* as a movement of stillness.

I'd like to share a personal experience, where I embarked on a shamanic journey following a deep calling. A highly respected shaman invited me to learn from him. We shared countless moments and he became, without a doubt, a guiding light, revealing the great flow of shamanism, a fresh, powerful, and deep current that captivated me for three fundamental reasons. First, its unwavering honesty. Shamans don't pretend to be better than anyone, they have no useless desires of ego in spiritual superiority with other beings or creatures. Shamans show themselves as they are, they allow their light and their shadow to come out, they recognize the most subtle and primal aspects of themselves. They dance in harmony with all living beings.

The second quality of shamanism that captivated me was the depth of the magical connection, understanding that everything is imbued with life: trees have consciousness and spiritual intelligence; we can feel the stars' pulse, even from the earth; we can connect with the spirits of the sea and the river, with the father sun and the lord of the wind. In fact, all of creation vibrates with energy and information. Learning to connect with this invisible plane was fascinating for me because, perhaps due to my clairvoyant abilities, although I perceived all these beings, it was not until I learned shamanism that I was able to truly understand them and establish two-way bonds, a true relationship of affection and respect, a dialogue with the invisible world.

The third element that completed my incessant search for a spiritual path coherent with who I am was joy. Shamanism celebrates pleasure and laughter. It is believed that joy is a spiritual force as important as love or peace. Color, spontaneity, singing, and dancing are embraced. One can play and then return to seriousness, enjoy food, share a song, rejoice in a poem, chase a butterfly—all while experiencing spirituality in a beautiful way.

Thus, I could summarize that my experience with shamanism was an encounter with honesty and essence, magic and transcendence, joy and life.

The first time I heard the concepts that would later become part of my own being, I could not integrate them. I was raised in a very different environment than most shamans. Growing up, I was far removed from the mountains, rivers, and lakes that have shaped the ancestral traditions of shamanism, often referred to as the "Red Road."

When I delved into the experience of shamanic initiation, everything seemed so distant, so alien, so out of this reality. It was as if I had stepped into a surrealist painting and, although it called to me and seemed fascinating, I had nothing with which to fit it into the history, both social and psychic, in which I had grown up.

I gradually realized that deep shamanism wasn't just a concept—it had to become part of my body, expressed in my words, and deeply rooted in my heart. I learned shamanism in the mountains of Chiapas, the sierras of Jalisco and Zacatecas, the jungles of Yucatán, and the Peruvian Apus mountains. I encountered it in the Canadian snow, and then it became so pervasive that, wherever I went, I found it, felt its spirit, and sensed its presence.

The first time I heard of ollin, it seemed like a very abstract concept. But let me share how I came to understand it.

One day, I was with my teacher atop a mountain. As we stood there, gazing out at the valley during that magical hour of dusk when day and night intertwine, he said, "Life sings." In that moment of profound awareness, I began to hear the soft murmur of the clouds in the sky. For the first time, I sensed the mountains singing. It wasn't the wind—it was a melody rising from those lofty peaks. Then, like a distant mantra, I heard the trees of various species humming a lullaby. The earth resonated deeply, like a drum. The water seemed to speak words I couldn't comprehend, yet I felt their presence. It was fascinating to hear the world's symphony, to sense that everything was alive and in perfect harmony. It was like a small orchestra where each creature's unique sound blended seamlessly, creating a natural, harmonious whole.

By perceiving this music, I learned that everything in the universe has a perfect rhythm, a grand symphony to which we can all contribute. When you align yourself with this universal rhythm, you become a part of it. This concept is somewhat similar to the Principle of Oneness, but it goes further—you can actively participate in the world's music, harmonizing your actions with the greater cosmic melody.

Ollin, as I was taught, is a rhythm, a pulse that connects us to creation and our desires. If, for example, you wish to find love using resonance and dharma, you must attune yourself to the rhythmic patterns of the universe. However, without understanding the timing and circumstances that are conducive to love, your search may be filled with obstacles. When you align your actions with the cosmic rhythm, love can flow into your life seamlessly.

Let's explore this example further. For love to blossom, both partners need to be on the same page. You might be deeply in love, but if they aren't feeling it, the relationship won't progress. You may be full of desire and the best intentions, but although it may be your time, it may not be the other person's. Or, on the contrary, the other person might be ready to commit, yet you may be distracted by other things—like a toxic relationship. Love only flourishes when both individuals are open and ready.

Sometimes, one person needs to wait. The other might need to let go of past relationships to make space for a new love. Ultimately, love can only truly blossom when both partners are open and willing. If you're young and seeking a serious relationship, you might need to wait until you're at a stage in life where you're more mature, and thus ready to connect deeply with someone.

I firmly believe that some couples find success because they met at exactly the right time. Perhaps this wonderful relationship you have with an older man or a fifty-year-old woman would have been impossible when you were only fifteen years old. Sometimes, we need to go through separations, divorces, or even losses before we can find someone who truly resonates with us and aligns with our life's rhythm. This is when a genuine love connection can blossom.

There's a perfect time for everything. A time to let go, to feel passion, to find solitude, to connect with yourself, and to share with a loved one. A time to be present and a time not to be. A time to draw near and a time to give space for love to oxygenate. Understanding these rhythms, this perfect synchronicity, is to understand the concept of ollin.

Let's return to the story of the mountain and my mentor.

The world is constantly singing to us. Sometimes, its song to you is, "It's time to produce and work, to build your dreams." If you listen to that song and align yourself with its energy, you'll find that everything falls into place.

But then the song of life changes. It says, "Now is the time for gratitude, silence, and introspection." If you ignore this song and continue to strive for recognition, you'll find less success, as the time has shifted. Moreover, you won't be able to enjoy the peace of inner reflection.

It's crucial to understand that life has its own rhythm, marking times for growth, creation, and dreaming, as well as times for receiving and honoring all that comes our way. Just as there are times for vacations, vigils, pregnancy, focused attention, and exercise, we must learn to recognize the cycles of peace and seeking, exploration and settling. There's a time for eating and digesting, for emptying and cleansing, for hunger and hydration. Every process has its perfect moment. The concept of ollin teaches us to "listen to the world's rhythm and find your perfect timing to live and do." In shamanic traditions, we're guided toward a paused, tranquil movement, a stillness.

Just as clouds drift serenely across the sky or water cascades effortlessly over a waterfall, there's a perfect rhythm to nature's movements. Nothing is rushed; everything has its perfect time. When you are fortunate enough to see a wildcat running freely, you can see how its movement, although fast, has a perfect rhythm. The moon, as it traverses the night sky, offers a similar sense of steady, timeless motion. This is ollin.

Our task is to discover our unique purpose, to understand the rhythm the universe has set for us now, and to align our inner rhythms with this cosmic dance. It's like being part of a grand ballet where music, steps, setting, and heartbeat move in perfect synchrony.

Tuning In

Dear reader, we've come a long way together. Consider where you are in your life as you read this fundamental principle.

What role does ollin play for you right now?

Perhaps you've noticed subtle signs from the universe, guiding you. As you learned about generation, maybe a part of you yearned for this understanding. And when you discovered dharma, you might have made some positive changes.

Now, as we explore the music of the world, I invite you to pause and reflect, asking: "What is the purpose of my life now? What steps should I take next? What is meant for me at this moment?"

Allow yourself to tune in to a deep inner knowing, like a gentle breeze, and discover your unique rhythm within the universe's grand melody.

ZEN AND THE RHYTHM OF THE UNIVERSE

A few years ago, I was fortunate enough to travel to Japan with some of my students. Among the many spiritual traditions of that beautiful country, I encountered Zen.

Zen is a spiritual path that invites us to contemplate ollin, time, harmony, and beauty. Within this tradition, you'll find poems of profound beauty and meaning. One such poem has stayed with me ever since I recited it in the ancient Japanese forests of Nara. I'd like to share it with you now. As you listen, savor each word, finding the pauses that give the poem its rhythm. Try to visualize each image and let the beauty and harmony of the lines sink into your soul.

It goes like this:

In spring, hundreds of flowers,
In autumn, the harvest moon,
In summer, a refreshing breeze,
In winter, snow blankets us.

If you can delve into the depths of this passage, you'll discover that each season has its own rhythm. It's futile for spring flowers to bloom in winter, and it's just as foolish for autumn to cling to its leaves, or for summer to try to block out the light of the sun.

Likewise, in our lives, we need to learn to observe ourselves and notice the many subtle shifts happening within us. Ask yourself: Is this a time for silence or for speaking up? Should I stay in or go out? Should I indulge or exercise restraint? Is this a time for power or humility? By paying attention to these questions, you'll find yourself flowing more easily with life, as you and the universe collaborate on something truly magnificent.

For those of us who practice shamanism, we learn to listen to the songs of the universe. We learn to discern when it tells us "Move forward," or "Shine brightly," but it's also crucial to recognize when it says "Stop." Nature is always communicating with us. A new moon signifies a new beginning, while a full moon signifies it's time to radiate. High tides invite us to set sail, while low tides remind us to be patient. Rain urges us to seek shelter, and cool mornings invite us on serene walks. A wet floor warns us to be cautious, and tall grass reminds us to watch our step.

Now, expand your perspective and pause to reflect: What is life inviting you to experience right now? What do you truly yearn for? And does your desire align with the rhythm that life is setting for you? When someone is too young and tries to live like an adult, something inevitably happens to show there's a disconnect. It's not a good look for a young person to play at being grown up, or for an elderly person to pretend to be a rebellious teenager. I'm not talking about a young person maturing or an older person feeling youthful—but simply about rhythm, timing, and the perfect harmony of the universe.

As you reflect, notice how many precious things in your life have come at just the right time. If you got married at the right time, for instance, that is reflected in the love and duration of your marriage, and your home arrives at its perfect moment. Perhaps you spent years chasing a job that never materialized, but maybe you learned to wait, practiced a little wu wei, understood you had to let go and be brave. When the opportunity finally aligned, you resonated with it, and it has unfolded beautifully.

We must often pause when we're consumed by anger and ask ourselves if this is the time for peace. When our hearts are broken, can we open ourselves to healing? Does our frantic pace align with the serene life we desire?

The Principle of Ollin teaches us to go with the flow. If a relationship isn't meant to be right now, it's important to accept it peacefully and wait for the right time. While this might seem similar to wu wei, there's a crucial difference. Wu wei is about trusting in the natural flow of life, while ollin is about actively participating in that flow. It's like listening to a song and waiting for your cue to join in. It is not only about your energy, as in the Principle of Generation, nor is it about letting life act, as in wu wei. Ollin is an intermediate point; I know what I have to do, but I pause, carefully waiting for the precise moment to be able to do it.

We've all heard tales of athletes who jumped the gun and failed, businesspeople who rushed to market and lost everything, songs that would have been real hits but were ahead of their time, or artists and geniuses who spoke with great truth to a world that simply was not ready to listen to them. On the flip side, there are those who waited too long to say "yes," and lost love, or had ideas that were shelved and forgotten, so much so that when they emerged there was no one left to appreciate them.

Imagine life as a grand symphony or a collection of smaller tunes. The rhythms of ollin imply different times—perhaps a time for love or for learning. Mornings might be for action, while nights for contemplation. Meals can be filled with laughter, yet dinners may offer moments of deep pauses.

The key is to learn to discern what the world is communicating and where you fit in to this grand scheme. There's another dimension to ollin—finding your place in the perfect moment, allowing things to unfold in the most harmonious way for the greater good.

Imagine a family photo. You're a guest or a close friend in this picture—you understand that you might not be the center of the picture. If you're mindful and have a sense of balance, you'll know your place. But if you ignore these concepts and constantly seek the spotlight, you'll create chaos. Nature and life operate on principles of order and harmony. Don't try to be someone you're not—it will lead to disorder. You don't need to be your wife's son or your husband's mother-in-law. Be a mother to your children, not their therapist. And remember, you're a patient to your therapist, not a friend. It's about finding your place in life and knowing when to act—that's true greatness and awareness—and when you do, life will have a way of rewarding you.

Let's consider a funny scenario. Imagine someone visiting a very cold country in winter, a place known for its snow. They arrive dressed in shorts, a t-shirt, flip-flops, a cap, and sunglasses. When they step outside the airport, they're furious at how cold it is and upset about the snowfall. Who's to blame? The weather, which has been the same for millennia, or the person who clearly didn't pack for the climate?

Life is what it is, and it's up to us to adapt. We need to know to bundle up in winter and wear light clothes in summer. That's what ollin is about. Similarly, if you visit someone's home for the first time and behave rudely, demanding the best seat at the table, you can expect a cold reception the next time.

Ollin requires common sense, observation, and awareness.

Have you ever wondered why life doesn't always give you what you want? Why, when you're ready to fall in love, nobody seems to appear? Or why, when you're trying to go one way, life seems to push you in the opposite direction? And why is it that when you need to open a door, life closes it for you? Maybe it's not bad luck—perhaps you're simply not interpreting life's signals correctly. It's crucial to take time to reflect and understand this beautiful concept of ollin.

I've structured these principles in a specific order to help you become more aware. We start by recognizing our connection to something greater than ourselves. Then, we explore how we can use our energy to create the reality we desire. Next, we discover the power of resonance to attract positive experiences into our lives. After that, we delve into the concept of karma and the importance of taking action. Sometimes, the best course of action is to simply let go and allow life to unfold. This seventh principle is about finding balance and harmony. It's about learning to listen to the universe as a symphony, and to add your voice in synchrony, aligning your own desires with a greater purpose. When you can do this, life will open up in wonderful ways.

Ollin, a Nahuatl word, is often translated as "movement"—but not the mechanical motion of a locomotive or the clunky movements of a robot. It's a serene kind of movement, like the gentle swaying of leaves on a tree, ever at peace. It's the rhythmic rise and fall of ocean waves, the graceful glide of a turtle underwater, or the effortless flight of a seagull.

Notice how all these movements are synchronized, beautiful, and perfectly balanced. Each one of them is in an invisible but perfect interaction with a higher symphony. Watching whales swim or fish school together is simply breathtaking. Even a desert sandstorm, creating a breathtaking canvas as it engulfs everything in its path, or electrical storms that move with a sense of perfect timing and balance are a testament to nature's beauty. Now it's your turn to realize you're part of this universal dance, and find your place within it.

FINDING YOUR PERFECT RHYTHM

Why is it so hard to find our perfect rhythm? Ego and control—two words that are tragically ingrained in human beings and that often get us into trouble. When we let them take the wheel, we fall into the burning spiral they create and life becomes suffocating, everything gets distorted from the ego's perspective and a false sense of control. We become out of tune with the rhythm of the world, trying to force reality to conform to our expectations, and struggle desperately to impose our idea of how things should be; instead of accepting what is happening, we seek to recreate circumstances according to our judgment.

It's like wanting to wear shorts in the snow or complaining about mosquitos in the jungle. What else would you expect to find in such places? It may sound ironic, but people can be surprised by the strangest things. There are people who get pregnant and then say, "My, how a child changes your life!" Of course having a child dramatically changes your life. Shouldn't that be obvious?

When I'm caught up in ego and control, I demand that the world sing my tune simply because I want it to. But the world responds, "I can't do that. My song isn't just about you. I'm part of a grand melody that includes you and every other being." Sometimes our personal song is intertwined with our children, our work, and our life's purpose. We're not soloists; we're part of a great choir.

Dear reader, I believe now is the perfect time for you to

grasp these principles. Your journey of learning has reached its culmination—this is ollin.

Let's use cooking as an analogy. I have a dear Spanish student who makes incredible *paella*. But paella, like any great dish, needs time. If you try to rush the rice, turning up the heat, it won't cook properly. If you take the seafood out too soon, it will be undercooked. You might feel frustrated, angry, or upset, but he's taught me that a good paella takes time. It's ready when it's ready, whether that's at two, three, or four in the afternoon.

Think of your projects like a paella. They need time to simmer and develop. It's about finding the right pace, allowing life and your work to flow together.

Primitive humans had a much deeper connection with nature. They understood that some places were suitable for living and others weren't. In our time, people build houses in riverbeds or on the edges of eroding mountains. When these places inevitably give way, people often blame the world for their misfortune, failing to understand the natural order of things. Rivers will always return to their courses, and mountains will erode. It's not the river or the mountain's fault—the people who built there didn't respect nature's boundaries.

Similarly, we often cling to things that no longer serve us. A relationship that has run its course, our youthful appearance, or past achievements—we hold onto them with an almost desperate intensity. If we don't accept that change is inevitable and embrace the present, we'll find ourselves trapped in a cycle of disappointment and suffering. This is because we're resisting the natural flow of life and clinging to what *was* instead of embracing what *is*.

A great way to explore this principle further is to allow children to enjoy childhood, young people to embrace youth, adults to live fully in adulthood, and the elderly to savor old age. It's about being rebellious when it's time to rebel and wise when wisdom is needed, about playing when it's appropriate and delving deep when the moment calls for it.

There's no point in rushing through life. Instead, we need to pay attention to both our internal and external rhythms. Do you function better during the day or the afternoon? Or are you a night owl, like me? Does winter air invigorate you or irritate your throat? Does alcohol soothe or exacerbate your distress? Does your tendency to talk a lot open or close doors for you? This self-awareness is key to discovering your place in the world and aligning all aspects of your life.

There are both collective and family rhythms. Within our families, for instance, our children might be seeking new experiences and ready to leave home, while we ourselves may be seeking balance. Our mothers might be in a reflective phase, our brothers experiencing love, and we, personal growth. We must understand that even though we share our lives with others—children, parents, siblings, partners, colleagues—we don't all experience time and rhythm in the same way. Respecting and understanding these different rhythms is key to peace and harmony.

On a collective level, communities often go through cycles of renewal, much like a social spring. We crave change and innovation, eager to see new things emerge and thrive. However, there are also times when communities seek stability and protection, wishing to preserve what they have. The challenge lies not in the passage of time itself, but in our ability to adapt to these cycles. We must avoid pushing for change during periods of stability and, conversely, resisting change when it's time for renewal.

Imagine how much better your life could be if you found

your rhythm, your place in the world, and the perfect timing for everything.

We've gotten caught up in some strange ideas lately. It seems like no one wants to die. But that's contrary to the natural order of things. We all have to die to make way for new life. If you artificially postpone your death, you generate disorder and imbalance. If you cling to life too tightly, you will inflict pain not just for yourself but for the people who care about you. We should accept that death is a natural part of life and strive to live so fully that, when it's time to go, we can do so peacefully.

We also sometimes pretend that change happens much faster than it actually does. However, there are movements that are slow, almost imperceptible. Did you see your children grow a centimeter each month? No. They developed naturally, so gently and consistently that one day you suddenly realized how much they'd grown. It's a beautiful thing to witness—life without rushing, yet without stopping. We can aspire to understand this movement, to become part of it. This is ollin.

In the past, humanity faced periods of famine; now we practice intermittent fasting. There was a time when fasting was necessary, for practical or spiritual reasons. Today, we often overeat. It's not about restriction or indulgence, but about balance. There are times for feasts and times for frugality. We don't need to feast during times of mourning, nor do we need to suffer in times of joy.

It's only natural to lose our rhythm, our ollin, from time to time. To regain our balance, we must remember the grand melody and learn to listen not just with our ears, but with our hearts. We need to reconnect with our inner sense of timing, understanding where we are in the grand scheme of things. It's not about following a strict timeline or being confined to a place. Instead, it's about developing a personal rhythm, learning to recognize when the universe is calling us to expand, to move forward, to pause and reflect, or simply to be.

Once we start seeking our rhythm, whether through resonance or generation, life begins to assist us. The specific rhythm we desire—for instance, to find a great job—emerges because life accompanies, blesses, and works for us. Thus, instead of feeling we are alone in the search for our happiness, we feel life working alongside us, almost magically orchestrating positive outcomes. The universe responds effortlessly; everything seems to fall into place. We experience coherence, a balance of resonance, dharma, generation, oneness, wu wei, karma, and ollin.

Take a moment to appreciate the perfection of this very instant. You're receiving these messages at the exact time they're meant to be received.

Some people have a natural knack for navigating life. They know how to save for a rainy day and savor the good times. They've learned the value of prosperity and know how to make the most of it. However, many people become complacent during prosperous times and are ill-prepared when hard times hit. I'm not just talking about finances, but also about relationships. These people neglect their closest connections and find it too late to repair the damage. Parents, for instance, might prioritize work over their children and regret it when their kids grow up and move on.

It's not uncommon to meet someone who has worn their body down to the point of exhaustion, only to realize they want to enjoy life when it's too late. Or someone who wastes their days watching TV and engaging in negativity, only to look back and realize they've squandered precious time.

That's why I invite you to pay attention to your rhythms,

understand the passage of time, and recognize your place in the world. Just as there are times for celebrations, laughter, and tears, there are times for everything in your life. Instead of getting upset that there's no snow in the rainforest, learn to appreciate the rainforest for what it is. And when you are in a place where the snow does come, enjoy that too.

The best advice I can give you is to listen to the rhythm of life's songs. When you make that rhythm a part of your heart, you'll find yourself moving in harmony with the universe and experiencing greater happiness.

THE FIVE KEYS OF OLLIN

Having spent considerable time experiencing and understanding ollin, I delved deeper into the symbolic and mystical knowledge hidden within the shamanic tradition—its stories, myths, foundations, and dances. I discovered that ollin is composed of five fundamental keys. By grasping these, we can fully appreciate the beauty and grandeur of this Universal Law.

1. Everything is part of a greater order. Chaos is merely a construct of the ego. Some people believe reality is defined by their ego's perception, rather than the true experience of the spirit.

For instance, many perceive old age as chaotic and filled with suffering. However, old age is simply a different phase of life, devoid of inherent negativity. When people label menopause as a "serious disease" without understanding it as a natural part of life, their perception, rather than the experience itself, contributes to their suffering. Similarly, a retiree might lament their early retirement, while another might resist the idea entirely.

The point is to understand that there is no such thing as chaos.

What we perceive as disorder and suffering is simply a reflection of our limited understanding. From a higher perspective, everything has a purpose and a place.

A pandemic, for instance, catches us off guard. We're a society that values appearances over substance, paying athletes exorbitant sums while neglecting our scientists. Then we're surprised when we face global crises. We prioritize exotic vacations over understanding ourselves, which only contributes to further chaos. But in reality, these events—pandemics, diseases, social unrest—serve a purpose. They challenge us to grow, learn, and rediscover attributes of our humanity that we had forgotten.

Remember that the universe has its own Grand Design, a cosmic chessboard where everything unfolds as it should. If you don't like it, or perceive that you live in too much chaos, you must go deep, inward, to the beginning of generation, and then discover that when you find inner peace, when you are in balance and equilibrium, you can join by resonance to the perfect movement—that is ollin.

2. Events are causal, not coincidental. There's no such thing as luck. As Einstein said, "God doesn't play dice." Everything in the universe is connected. Every event has a cause, the Principle of Karma. This cause can be positive and beneficial—dharma, or a vibration we attract by resonance. Remember, events are causal, not coincidental. The concept of ollin helps us understand that every situation carries a message. We should ask: Is this the right moment? Where do I fit in? How can I peacefully adapt to this new flow?

3. Everything is part of a process. When we view death as an end, we often feel anger and sadness. We fight against it. Similarly, we see economic crises as isolated events, and we suffer and cling to the idea that the economy has to be always abundant. We perceive loss as a failure and unconsciously resist it. We usually look at only a small fragment of reality.

It's like judging an entire movie based on a single screenshot. We need to realize that life isn't a series of disconnected fragments but a continuous process, much like karma. Instead of viewing events as beginnings or endings, we should see them as part of an endless flow. Once we understand that death is simply a transition to a new life and crises are opportunities for growth and learning, we'll realize nothing happens in isolation. Every event has a purpose.

When I travel, I'm so grateful for the existence of places untouched by tourism, far from roads and train tracks. To reach them, I often have to hike and carry my backpack to places without air conditioning or television. This "lack of development" is what keeps these places pure. But when highways are built, internet and cable TV are installed, and hotels pop up, some of that purity is lost. If I thought something was inherently wrong with a place lacking in modern conveniences, this would be a distorted view. I can appreciate the beauty of innocence, whether in a place or a person. Just as a road will eventually be built, I understand that innocence will fade. But until then, I cherish the journey on the dirt road.

Moments both good and bad are interconnected, part of a continuous flow of energy, a cyclical pattern. It's essential to understand that everything is part of a journey. As a collective, humanity needs these experiences, and as individuals we must learn from them. All that is happening, whether positive or challenging, is part of a process we must navigate and understand. The sooner we grasp the lesson and align ourselves with the rhythm of life, the smoother our journey will be. It's not about whether things are good or bad, but about what we learn from them. Life is about lessons, not rewards or punishments.

4. We live in a state of impermanence. This concept is deeply rooted in Buddhist philosophy. It teaches us that everything is constantly changing and evolving. For instance, you might wish your children would stay young forever, but they'll continue to grow. Or you might long for happy moments to last eternally, but even joy is fleeting. When you try to rush or slow down life's pace, remember that everything happens in its own time. Impermanence reminds us not to cling too tightly to either the "very good" or "very bad" things.

There's a timeless saying, "This too shall pass." It's a simple phrase, yet profound. Change and impermanence are a substantial part of the order of things and, as ollin suggests, just as there are beginnings, there are endings. Just as there is hope, there is acceptance. Gains and losses are part of life. And everything, ultimately, is both impermanent and perfect as it is. Both the good and the bad will pass; once you embrace this idea, you'll find a deep sense of peace.

5. The universe has a perfect rhythm. Imagine a grand melody playing throughout all existence. It's a force, an energy. How we each interpret this is important, but what truly matters is understanding the underlying order, the cosmic score that orchestrates oneness. This score is dictated by a higher consciousness. When we learn to tune in to it and discover our place within it, we flow through life with joy and fulfillment. Everything has its season—fulfillment and calm, pregnancy and death, uncertainty and sadness. We are part of a cycle of love and solitude, companionship and introspection. There are times of opulence and times of humility and simplicity. Time to sing to children when they are small and time to embrace their departure when they grow up. There is time to work and time to enjoy work, to travel and to be present. There is time to raise children and time to respect their adult decisions.

Time to say "no" and time to accept the inevitability of life.

So, what's the problem? Why can't we see the bigger picture? Our egos often get in the way. We want a new car right now, without considering if it's the right time. We want children on our own terms, disregarding the deeper meaning and timing of life. We demand that our orchids bloom year-round, forgetting that even plants have their own cycles and we must treat them with affection, waiting for them to grow again.

Therefore, we must learn to live in rhythm with ollin. We must read between the lines, just as we look to the sky to predict rain, we must look beneath the surface of behaviors, signs, and synchronicities. We must understand that after rain comes drought and vice versa. We must realize that every journey must have a return, and that by being mindful, we can anticipate the night. We tend to resist the understanding that there are phases of life—childhood, adolescence, old age, and death. When we fight against these cycles, we only suffer, not because of the cycles themselves, but because of our attachment and stubbornness.

Perhaps when it was your time to love, you prioritized your career, earning a comfortable living. But when you finally returned to love, the person you cared about was no longer there. Or maybe you chose love over work, only to find that love faded when money became scarce. The point is, life is a continuous flow, and we must learn to balance love and work. There are times for both, and times for rest and reflection—like reading this very book. I hope you're finding it both enjoyable and enriching.

You must learn to live in harmony, just like a ship navigating waves. Embrace fullness and beauty while recognizing and working through challenging times. Cherish abundance but always prioritize what truly matters. Remember, you're like a ship and you must learn to read the tides, make choices, and even anticipate what's to come. To do this, stay present and listen to your heart. Uncover the falsehoods of promises like "money equals happiness" or "a degree guarantees success." In reality, understanding Universal Laws, connecting with peace and calm, and knowing, respecting, and loving yourself is far more valuable than material possessions or academic achievements.

Therefore, I invite you to observe yourself closely. If you have people who love you and it's time to love, love. Instead of arguing with your partner or deciding to do something different, when it's time to love, love. When it's time to work, work, and when it's time to find peace, live in peace. Nothing is more distressing and sadly more common than someone sitting on a beach with a computer in front of them, unable to look at the sea, thinking about their Tuesday meeting—or someone who is in that meeting on Tuesday but is mentally connected to the waves.

Let's be mindful. Let's learn to live in the moment, whether we're at sea, in the office, in love, or facing our limits.

I'm sure you've experienced times when you were supposed to keep the peace but ended up arguing, which ended in conflict. Or maybe you've butted in to conversations when you should have just listened, and ended up causing chaos. Let's respect boundaries, both in our homes and in our relationships. Let's embrace each season for what it offers. And let's remember to balance our lives, making time for work, rest, and joy.

It's not just about achieving one goal, but about living a full and balanced life. The happiest people aren't just those who have reached the pinnacle of their careers. They're the ones who have strong relationships, fulfilling work, recognition, abundance, inner peace, good health, and joy. A little bit of everything in its right measure.

INTEGRATING OLLIN

To discover ollin, you must recognize there are two movements. The internal, guided by your heart, which tells you if it is your time or not. And the external, occurring in the world around you, allows you to read the world, anticipating events like an approaching storm or a hot day. For ollin to be balanced, you must delve into your intuition. Meditation can help you connect with your inner wisdom. But you must also learn to listen to the orchestra of the world around you, to discover the rhythm and find your place within it.

While it may seem complex, it's actually quite natural. Intuitively, we follow the rhythms of day and night, and we understand the progression from childhood to adulthood. Trust your inner guidance and pay attention to what's happening around you. It's like you have an inner melody waiting to harmonize with the eternal symphony of the universe.

Ollin is about listening to your intuition and aligning with the flow of life. When you end a relationship at the right time, choose peace over conflict, recognize when it's time to generate or simply embrace silence, you're living in harmony with ollin. When you handle disagreements with wisdom, stand up for what's right, and respect the feelings of those you love, you're embodying ollin.

Have you ever noticed how some people always seem to make the perfect requests? They ask in a way that makes it impossible to say no. These are people who start a business at the perfect moment to generate abundance or who offer you help at exactly the time you need it. When I was giving consultations, there were people who had to wait six or seven months to get an appointment because I was completely booked, but there were some clients who wrote to me just when someone had canceled or who had a perfect knack for finding me with my agenda in hand, and for some reason, I would give them a consultation in less time. That is rhythm, not luck. There are people who deliver the right project at the right time and achieve success, by learning to read the universe. Once you learn to interpret the signs and ride the waves of life, you'll experience a sense of effortless flow.

If you adopt this approach, dear reader, and integrate it into your life, if you pay close attention to your inner guidance and stay aligned with it, you'll gradually discover your place in the grand symphony of the universe—you'll become part of ollin. You will then discover that life can be effortless, with the universe's tides guiding you toward your highest potential. Embracing the ollin in your life means transitioning from being stubborn to becoming a fluid wind that always blows in the optimal direction.

Since ollin came into my life, I've gained a deeper understanding of time and its rhythms. It has brought me incredible rewards, allowing me to patiently wait for the right moments both for others to be receptive to my message and for me to connect with the perfect people. Whenever I face challenges or complexities, I pause to consider what this moment requires. The more I listen to my heart and recognize my place in the world, the more beautiful life becomes.

Perhaps it's time for you to close this book, reflect, and look around. Maybe it's time to make a change, or perhaps to dive deeper into another principle. I know my words are right for you at this moment. You and I, without having met face to face, belong to the oneness and are creating ollin because, by reading my book, you allow me to continue advancing in the fulfillment of my dreams, and I, by writing this for you, perhaps can give you a spark or a push so you can go live the beautiful life you deserve.

Life is full of energy, and it's essential to let that energy flow as it should. Ollin is about understanding these flows, embracing them, and aligning with them for our greatest good—that's what this is all about. Whether it's time to end a relationship, let go of a fight, or stand up for what you believe in—ollin is all about timing. It's about knowing when to connect with friends and when to give them some space. Ever noticed how some people seem to have naturally good timing for everything? They know when to call, when to listen, and when to let go. Others, however, seem to always be out of sync, causing unnecessary stress and conflict. This lack of harmony is the opposite of ollin. People who make thoughtful requests are a pleasure to be around.

Well-timed ollin will inevitably lead us to a more peaceful life. Think of a surfer waiting for the perfect wave. They can't just jump on any wave, but they also can't miss opportunities, because then they will never get to stand on their board. They know how to surf, trust their board, and time their rides perfectly. When the surfer and wave align, magic happens. Similarly, a skilled musician becomes one with the melody and never goes out of tune. For the surfer, it's the wave and his technique; for the musician, his work and the music itself. It's about harmony—timing, skill, and being in the right place at the right time.

By embracing the concept of ollin deep in our hearts instead of blindly following the crowd like sheep, we can align ourselves with the natural rhythms of life. We are not just sheep, and we also do not blindly do what others tell us we should do. On the contrary, we ask ourselves and understand what our moment and place is. Thus, we go through life acting based on that understanding and from a deep coherence with ourselves and the world around us.

When it comes to our children and close relationships, this conscious and loving approach is invaluable. We could learn to ask ourselves if our words will add value. We could try to understand what they're going through rather than judging them. We could coexist in a peaceful and harmonious way, guided by love. When we respond in a timely and appropriate manner, those around us can sense it. Our words—whether advice, comments, or even gentle reprimands—will resonate differently when they're delivered at the right moment.

We need to learn when it's time to let go. When our message isn't being received, perhaps because of a lack of readiness or the right words, we need to trust there's a better time and place. That's the magic of letting go—seeking out a more favorable moment. The universe aligns with those who harmonize with its flow. It offers loving support to those who open their hearts and embrace its rhythm.

When I understand ollin, that perfect movement, it guides me effortlessly.

Meditation for Synchronicity

This is a meditation for reclaiming our synchronicity with time and our dance with it.

Close your eyes and get comfortable, feeling present in this moment.

Listen to your breath, a gentle guide leading you back to yourself. Breathe in and out calmly. Feel the stillness and the peace. Relax your shoulders, release your abdomen, and exhale, letting go. Now, perceive a great calmness with each inhale, breathing in stillness and serenity.

Bring all your attention to your heart.

Visualize a bright point in the core of your heart and feel the deep calm of breathing and living here.

Exhale calmly, taking all the time you need, learning to know yourself in this meditation.

Open your mouth slightly, drop your jaw a little, and inhale and exhale through your nose. Allow your heart to continue finding more and more peace.

Now, notice what life is telling you.

Your life, your relationships, your body, everything matters. Ask yourself: What is this time for? Is this time for myself? Or is this time for what surrounds me? Is it a time for inward reflection or outward expansion? A time for creation or contemplation? Is it time for hot sunlight or cool weather? Is it time to spend or save? Is it time to be silent or to speak up? Is it time to disconnect or respect? Is it a time of doing? Is it a time of helping or of setting limits?

Now, listen to the sound of the mantra and start letting go of your thoughts.

Free your mind and let the sound of the mantra integrate with your breath, showing you from within, healthily, what this time is about. Your breath flowing peacefully with the sound flowing peacefully with your breath.

Relax your hands and let these affirmations resonate in your mind:

- *I surrender to the perfect flow of life.*
- *I trust in the wisdom of the universe.*
- *I am at peace.*

Take nine deep, calming breaths.

There is no path to peace, peace is the path.

GANDHI

Universal Law VIII

Peace

Peace is more than a word or an emotion;
it's a way of life, a state of consciousness.

I grew up with a deep-rooted belief in a Higher Power that listened and responded. From a very young age, I experienced beautiful spiritual connections. I've felt cherished and guided by the divine since I can remember. I've mostly dedicated my life to spirituality. Yet, at nineteen I faced a crisis unlike any other. In my despair, I challenged the divine. Like a petulant child, I questioned the Higher Power: "Why don't you love me? Why do bad things happen to good people like me? Why have you forsaken me? Why couldn't you prevent this pain?" I plunged into a deep depression.

A few weeks passed and, by fate and ollin, I found myself on the beach, pacing back and forth. I walked the beach from one end to the other several times. After about three or four hours, as my mind wandered I reflected on how difficult my current situation was and, through tears, I tried to find some answers. Looking out at the sea, I cried out, "Answer me!" My voice grew stronger, more insistent. "Answer me, I need to hear you!"

Throughout my life, I haven't always heard an audible voice from above. Instead, I've received higher messages through my intuition, often in the form of symbols, signs, images, feelings, or incidents. But this time I yearned for a direct answer, so I cried out, "Answer me!" As I wept, I thought, *If you don't answer now, I'll leave you and resent you. Maybe if you don't answer me as I need, it's because you don't exist.*

And the Higher Power remained silent . . .

Suddenly, I became aware that this lack of answer was because I was not really asking anything, I was just arguing.

In a moment of clarity, I asked two questions that I'm only now fully grasping. From the turmoil of my teenage years, I asked, "Will I ever be truly happy?" And then, "Does true happiness even exist?"

The once-turbulent sea abruptly stilled, creating a moment of suspended animation. A powerful voice then boomed from the sky, "True happiness is peace."

While I didn't fully grasp its meaning at the time, I started to prepare myself to unravel this mystery and its answer, which filled my heart with calm. This extraordinary experience marked a turning point in my life. Despite the fact that perhaps I did not fully understand the answer, a space opened up in me that would gently prepare itself to understand that true happiness exists and that it is called peace.

A few years later, perhaps eight or ten, I finally understood—happiness is a result of peace. To experience lasting joy, I had to find inner peace first. And just as that divine voice on the beach had revealed, true happiness is nothing more than peace.

Peace is something that sprouts, that arises. People often seek it out, spending countless hours in meditation or study, trying to extract it from ancient texts or rituals. But true peace emerges spontaneously, like a spring bubbling up from the earth. Certain factors can foster this inner peace.

When we're in ollin, in harmony with the universe, or when our actions align with dharma, and we radiate light from generation and peace arises naturally. And as peace emerges, desires, arrogance, and the need for things to be different—taller or shorter, larger or smaller—simply vanish. Everything feels perfect just as it is.

We discover peace when we fully accept the universe as it is. This deep state of tranquility arises from the understanding that the universe is inherently perfect and harmonious. Surprisingly, we realize peace is the natural state of all beings and creation.

Life is transformed when it springs from peace. A desire born of calm and quiet carries immense power. This happens when you recognize peace as a human experience, seeing it in the singer's voice, the sleeping baby, the meditating mystic, and even the reveler.

Peace can be active or passive, but it is present when we're truly ourselves, without the need to feign or pretend. A child allowed to be themselves will naturally express peace. A loved pet will live in harmony. A tree or a mountain, simply being, embodies peace.

Peace isn't about stillness or boredom; it's about accepting life as it is. It's the serenity of a tree, the joy of a dog napping, the contentment of a sleeping baby. By embracing who we are and what is, we can expand the peace that flows through us.

Nature is peaceful. A child is born into peace, and human beings die in peace. But this peace is disrupted when we fill ourselves with thoughts of lack, need, and desire—all stemming from the ego. Death is painless, and birth is serene. It's when we start forming assumptions and desires that we begin to judge and crave, caught in unhealthy attachments that rob us of our peace.

A child finds joy in singing until someone tells them they're singing off-key and need to improve. Children are happy dressing however they please until they're told it's wrong or inappropriate. That's where we start losing our peace—when we abandon our natural selves, pretending to be someone we're not, all in the hope of gaining acceptance or something else.

Peace is living with calm and presence, being part of goodness, and striving for the well-being of all.

Peace does not require embellishments or additions. It is simply calm and serenity, presence and love. We're not talking about possessing all luxuries or demanding that everyone we care about is happy or that our surroundings are perfect. Nor are we discussing political changes or the intensity of the sunlight that comes through our window. We're saying that peace is a state of calm and presence, regardless of external circumstances. Peace is a choice and, as I mentioned earlier, a state of mind.

If our peace depends solely on our surroundings being ideal, then it's not truly peace. We must learn to find peace within ourselves, regardless of our circumstances.

We can find solace in the following teaching: "Seek refuge within yourself when faced with life's storms and vicissitudes." Peace is that sanctuary, the ability to close our eyes, connect with our true self, and remain undisturbed. Imagine a deep, inner sanctuary that keeps you safe and protected—that is peace.

HOLDING PEACE IN HARD TIMES

What can we do when life gets tough and we lose our peace? If finances are strained, you can take the necessary steps—job hunting, debt restructuring, saving. And even if we can't solve everything at once, we can find peace by approaching the situation calmly and mindfully. If we're diagnosed with an illness, we can seek medical advice and follow treatment—while also cultivating inner peace, with calm and mindfulness. When we lose a loved one, it is natural to grieve. Yet, we can grieve with calm and mindfulness, knowing that deep down, beneath the surface, there is peace to be found.

When you put a lot of effort into a project that doesn't pan out, it's important to cultivate calm and mindfulness as you accept this frustration. These are essential tools for living a truly spiritual life. The more you cultivate inner calm and presence, the deeper your understanding of peace will become. You'll begin to see how peace, as a spiritual experience and state of mind, benefits everyone.

A person at peace seeks the well-being of themselves and others. They don't harbor ill will or envy, nor do they judge or criticize. When you live in peace, you stop interfering in the lives of others. You focus on your own inner calm, and as it grows, it naturally extends to those around you, inviting them to experience peace as well.

It's healthy to realize that when we experience love, peace, and mindfulness within ourselves, when we're truly present in that moment, we naturally desire that same experience for all beings. As I've mentioned, peace is our natural state. It's the essence beneath the flower, the look in your dog's eyes, the stillness of a sleeping child. To find peace, we simply need to connect with that deep, transcendent part of ourselves. Without forcing anything, we allow peace to arise, to blossom, and to manifest.

AN INNER SPIRITUAL SANCTUARY

Undoubtedly, among the spiritual laws I've presented, peace is the highest aspiration. If you understand this, you'll see that it's deeply connected to dharma and ollin. Where there's peace, there's no conflict, no chaos. Only light.

My aim in writing this book is to guide you in creating a spiritual sanctuary, a place of retreat and evolution, so when you go out into life you can understand that everything is unified, everything is interconnected. You understand and acknowledge that you are a generator of what is happening in that interconnectedness, and you play an active role in shaping your reality. You are a vibrational being, attracting what you put out, and these vibrations interact with you and with those around you. By cultivating loving, kind, and coherent intentions, you can take responsibility for the causes you create and the effects you experience. Sowing seeds of light will bring positive changes into your life. I hope to help you find moments of peace and stillness, enabling you to recognize when it's time to move forward and live a life of tranquility. Ultimately, my goal is for you to truly feel and recognize peace.

I'd like you to return to this paragraph and recognize that you already possess the knowledge of these eight spiritual laws.

We can't live in a world where we feel the external is more powerful than the internal. We've already acknowledged that we are creators. If you generate abundance, success, health, love, and joy—all creation that stems from a central, bright, and peaceful part of you—I assure you that everything you build will yield magnificent results.

Peace isn't something we pretend to have or hope for in the future; it's a present-moment experience, something we cultivate daily. Living in peace does not exclude you from getting angry or frustrated, from having a tantrum or outburst—but the key is to recognize when you've lost your peace and quickly return to your center, your sanctuary, your calm. Meditation, prayer, nature walks, reading, and listening to uplifting content can help you cultivate a more peaceful state. Carefully choosing your friends, conversations, and daily activities can create a supportive network that helps you experience peace in all its forms.

Now it's your turn to examine your life. Make lists of your activities and consider whether they bring you closer to or further from peace. Imagine peace as a garden that needs tending. You must remove weeds and pests to ensure a healthy harvest. Therefore, if competition, ego, or other issues upset you or put you in a bad mood and disturb your peace, eliminate them. Your environment should support your inner peace and serenity, and your peace and serenity should benefit your surroundings. Peace comes from being true to yourself. Remember, it's a natural state—you don't need to do anything special, just be. Smile, close your eyes, breathe deeply—that's the start. I'll leave it to you to discover your path to lasting peace. You now have the tools to live fully and peacefully.

The Chains of Ignorance

A fulfilling life begins when we shed the ignorance that has been imposed upon us.

The Universal Laws we've learned are powerful tools. Yet, three chains of ignorance often hold us back from living in harmony, synchronicity, and fulfillment. The greatest poverty, spiritually speaking, isn't financial but a lack of consciousness.

When people have a limited understanding, they fall into a sad and gloomy life, unaware of what keeps them trapped and unable to evolve.

Among the many chains that limit our life three are essentially limiting, and we must learn to recognize them so they do not hinder us on our path to creating the life we want to experience.

These chains cause conflict, unhappiness, and chaos. They undermine and sometimes even corrupt the principles we've learned.

By understanding and overcoming these chains, we can create a harmonious and peaceful life.

THE FIRST CHAIN
MISCONCEPTION OF STRUGGLE AND SACRIFICE

The first chain is the misconception that life is all about struggle and sacrifice. This outdated belief suggests we must constantly fight and strive to achieve our goals. It promotes a mindset of constant vigilance to protect oneself from enemies and always keep one's guard up against perceived threats. This is a primitive way of thinking, akin to a caveman fiercely guarding a successfully hunted mammoth. Yet, a mammoth is too large for one person to consume, and any attempt to store it would lead to waste. Similarly, we often feel the need to protect our possessions and relationships, constantly battling external threats. This distorted view traps us in a state of perpetual tension and conflict, making us believe that pain, sacrifice, and fear are necessary for growth.

This way of thinking distorts our perception of life, making us believe that every day is a battle and we must always be armed. If we look around us, we'll find that many people are chained by this mindset, unable to let go, trust, or simply flow with life—as if denied the opportunity to experience the harmony and joy of dharma, the simple resonance, or the peaceful flow of ollin.

THE SECOND CHAIN
IMMEDIACY

The second chain is immediacy. Using only short-term thinking, we can't grasp the long-term consequences of our actions. We live in a world of instant gratification, where we consume everything as if there were no tomorrow, destroying everything without considering the future. Like buffaloes, we become fixated on the present, neglecting the broader perspective. This short-sightedness prevents us from perceiving life's full depth. It's what drives people to addictions, seeking instant rewards without considering the consequences. This inability to see the bigger picture, the transcendent, goes against the Principle of Karma. When we understand karma, we recognize that our actions have consequences. We see life as a series of causes and effects.

In this instant gratification mindset, I do whatever I please. No one sees me, I don't care, nothing matters. I can steal or cause damage with no repercussions. This immediacy is a disregard for responsibility. It's as if everything is permissible because I can't see the individuality or consequences of my actions. Impulsive thinking leads us to make decisions without considering their consequences for ourselves or others.

Another misconception that concerns me is the idea that spiritual awakening can happen instantly, like flipping a switch. Remember, spiritual growth is a journey, not a destination. It involves processes and cycles. Learn to embrace the flow of ollin to find inner peace.

Nothing happens by chance—everything is part of a grand cosmic process known as karma. It's up to you to weave these threads into a beautiful tapestry of your own spiritual awakening. By doing so, you can support those around you, live a life filled with love, and cultivate a deep sense of peace and belonging.

THE THIRD CHAIN
LIMITED PERCEPTION

The third chain is limited perception—believing life is superficial, viewing events as finalities, and forgetting oneness, vibration, and resonance. Spirituality consciously broadens our worldview, allowing us to see that everything has a cause and purpose. Our experiences are part of a deeper fabric of pulsations, energies, and intentions. The more spiritual we become, the less we're confined by assumptions, judgments, or superficial thinking. Breaking free from this limitation is like exploring the ocean's marvelous depths, not just its surface. This expands our lives.

These three chains of ignorance are interconnected. People who view life as a constant struggle tend to be selfish, feeling the need to protect their own interests. This selfishness often leads to a narrow-minded perspective, preventing them from taking responsibility for their actions or considering the long-term consequences.

I'm sure that if you examine your own behavior with honesty, you'll recognize instances where you've fallen into these patterns. You might think, "I want my life to improve, but I'm being selfish by wanting it to improve at the expense of others" or "I'm protecting what's mine because I feel threatened, and that makes me selfish and short-sighted."

We often find ourselves caught in a constant struggle, a battle to win, be better, and prove ourselves. This limited perspective traps us in an egocentric mindset, where we believe our judgments are always right and that the world must conform to our desires. We forget that the universe is vast, ancient, and infinitely wiser than we are. People often ask, "If I'm such a pure and good soul, why does everything go wrong for me?" This question leads to a wide range of often contradictory answers:

The universe is against me.
I've been hurt.

I'm a victim of my life's story.
My parents were terrible.
Life isn't fair.

It is much easier to say all this than to hold ourselves responsible, at least in part, for the reality we are living and co-creating.

Dear reader, can you identify these three chains of ignorance and stay alert so they don't ensnare you?

Life is meant to be lived freely. We don't need to be shackled. The result of consciousness is freedom.

Epilogue

Final Words

I grew up in a typical home, experiencing both challenging and joyful moments. My life was guided by ideas of struggle, effort, and thoughts that I later discovered were not so healthy. I had a mix of sweet and bitter experiences, yet I was also blessed with love, friendship, and happiness.

The concept of peace gradually unfolded for me through encounters with extraordinary, enlightened individuals. One of the most powerful moments in my life was in Arunachala, a sacred mountain in southern India. I was in search of an authentic saint, who I found after much persistence. He was sitting almost naked under a tree, and had been meditating for decades. I know it may be difficult for our busy minds to comprehend someone meditating for so long without basic needs like food or bathroom visits, but he was living proof.

That encounter was one of the greatest gifts of my life, a result,

I believe, of a dharma sown by deep love years ago. The atmosphere was almost indescribable—as sacred and peaceful as a temple despite being outdoors in a harsh, arid landscape with terrible heat. A profound peace radiated from that small, seemingly insignificant person. As I gazed upon him, his tranquility washed over me, allowing me to contemplate my life in resonance with his meditation. I was able to view my conflicts with others from a perspective I had never imagined. Suddenly, I could see clearly the relationships from throughout my life, and realized the person I believed had harmed me was simply another soul in the immense ocean of souls that evolve and were now incarnated here, doing the best they could in this lifetime, just as I was.

I spent hours there, gaining a profound and crystal-clear understanding of the experiences I had lived through. It was as if I were watching all the episodes of a great series, with a happy ending unfolding before my eyes. I felt an overwhelming sense of peace. From that moment on, something within me shifted. I stopped resisting. I began to accept and understand that while adversity was inevitable, I could navigate it from a place of deep calm, from a peaceful place.

Certainly, I've experienced loss, conflict, tears, and anger many times since then. But when I look within, I find peace beneath all that pain. I've been blessed to learn to live in peace, to make it my constant companion. I have managed to remain harmoniously at peace despite my life's circumstances, and this has filled me with love and gratitude for life. Today, many years after that profound experience of shouting at the beach when the divine answered me, I can confidently say that true happiness exists, and that it is, indeed, called peace.

I am so grateful you are part of this beautiful journey. I hope my words reach you and inspire you to seek a life of peace. When we've been given so much, we have a duty to share. It brings me joy to share these lines with you from a perfect rhythm and a good dharma. Now we resonate together and recognize ourselves as part of the oneness. We share the responsibility and an intention that everything always happens for a greater good. Remember, life is a constant song—but only when we're spiritually attuned can we hear its melody. And with love in our hearts and intentions, we can even help to write its next verse.

May the song of your life enrich the lives of those you love, and may you find happiness. Be true to yourself.

BOOKS OF RELATED INTEREST

Ancient Manifestation Secrets
Working with the 7 Laws of the Universe to Manifest Your Life and Purpose
by George Lizos
Foreword by Emma Mumford

Drawing on ancient Greek and Egyptian wisdom, George Lizos presents a 5-step process for successful manifestation by working with the laws of the Universe and your own energetic field. He also presents inner work practices for releasing cognitive and emotional blocks and limiting beliefs that hinder your manifestation journey.

Karma Healing
Unblock Your Life on the Soul Level
by Yael Eini

Exploring karma and its impact on our lives, Eini explains how to work through soul lessons, past life experiences, reincarnation patterns, and the karmic knots holding you back. She details Karmic Constellations, a method she developed, which combines energy healing and family constellations to intuitively engage with past lives and soul contracts.

Manifestation Perfected
Six Steps to Embody Your Soul Purpose
Baptist de Pape

Baptist de Pape looks at the lives of three of the most important personalities in the realm of manifesting—Oprah, J. K. Rowling, and Anita Moorjani. Following their examples, this book offers a clear and easy-to-follow series of six steps that anyone can adopt to become the master creator of their life and happiness.